Journeys
Through
the South

FRED POWLEDGE

Journeys
Through
the South

A Rediscovery

THE VANGUARD PRESS, INC.   NEW YORK

For PHYLLIS ABBOTT PEACOCK,
a Yankee who moved South to grow orchids,
all of which she gives away.

The idea for this book—for an examination of the modern-day South, based on a number of serendipitous journeys through the region—grew out of a series of twenty-six articles I wrote for *The Charlotte Observer*, and which appeared weekly from May 23 until November 13, 1977. The series was the conception of the *Observer*'s imaginative and highly professional editor, David L. Lawrence, Jr. I am deeply grateful to him for perceiving the need for such a series, for commissioning me to do it on a freelance basis, for encouraging me to go where I felt I should go and to write what I knew I should write, for extraordinarily sensitive editing (meaning he didn't change much), and for the frequent use of column-stretchers to get in all the words. Such editors are getting rare and ought to be protected.

I also am thankful to everyone else at *The Charlotte Observer* who helped with the series, including especially Dottie Adams, Robert De Piante, Stuart Dim, and Rolfe Neill.

FRED POWLEDGE

Contents

Contents

IV *Anticipation*

V *The harvest*

I
Preparations

1
Warmth

The gathering that New Year's Day was larger than any of its predecessors. The turnout had always been pretty good, but this time the people filled two floors of the old brownstone. It *sounded* like one of those parties we used to have years ago in Atlanta: the frequent laughter, much of it heavy and hearty and long and obviously sincere; the upraised voices, their volume violating all the rules of polite New York cocktail-party geography and carrying across the rooms and up and down the stairs; and most of all the mellowness of the accents, as out of place in this part of Brooklyn as an Alabama license plate.

It was an annual affair, a ritual consumption of Southern foods by some of us who live in New York and who still call ourselves Southerners. It started some years ago when I, a native Southerner married to a tolerant Chicagoan, and Kitty Terjen, an Atlantan married to Hank, a

Los Angeles native, decided to revive for ourselves the Southern tradition of eating hog jowls and black-eyed peas on the first day of the New Year. The mixture is believed by some Southerners to insure good luck for the entirety of the new year. Even if it doesn't, it's a good excuse for a party.

Gradually, the event and the number of people who were invited to it grew, until by this time, New Year's Day, 1977, it had become something of a feast. The hog jowls were authentic. They had been carried, frozen, by me past a confused airport security lady on the way back from a Southern trip. (One year we couldn't find any jowls, and I had to purchase half a hog's head from a nearby Puerto Rican butcher shop. The damned eye kept winking at me as I tried to extract some meat from the skull.)

Kitty had baked her usual outlandish number of pecan pies. Bob Ashton, a Wall Street lawyer who comes from Nashville, had sunk a terrifying amount of money into an authentic country ham and had it shipped to Brooklyn, and Jean Ashton, born in Detroit, had made a black-bottom pie. We had two kinds of cornbread as well as cornpone, collards, turnip greens, Savannah red rice, butterbeans, buttermilk, shrimp Creole. And, to make the feast authentic, we had RCs and Moon Pies.

Royal Crown Cola, the soft drink that every Southerner seems to remember from his or her youth, was locally available in Brooklyn. Moon Pies, or chocolate-covered wafers around a filling of white goo, were definitely not Brooklyn items, and a carton of the delicacies had surprised airport security even more than the frozen hog jowls. For Southerners who needed to cleanse their palates between courses, we had California wine.

The cheerfulness inside the house contrasted strongly with the rawness of the day outside. It was cloudy, cold, wet—fairly typical for early January in New York, which gets its only really interesting weather in the fall. Inside, Southerners and transplanted Southerners, exiled Southerners and self-exiled Southerners, along with a few Northern friends, warmed their hands and filled their stomachs in front of the fireplaces and talked with one another, almost exclusively about the South.

It had not been that way in earlier years. Before, when we would gather at our house or the Terjens', there would be talk about the South, but much of it would be token obligatory talk, summoned up just for the occasion by people who were Southerners, but for whom *being* Southerners had apparently ceased to have great meaning. We would go through the rituals with enthusiasm, but not necessarily with fervor. Upon being introduced to someone we had not met before, we would listen to the voice a moment and play the game of guessing their home state. And there would be great whoops of joy when the food was served—but the exclamations seemed a tad theatrical, coming as they did from people who had largely abandoned the tastes of their childhoods and who felt more comfortable now with Szechuan or Neapolitan delicacies.

The whole gathering, in fact, was more of a theatrical occasion than the coming together of a group of people linked by an almost religious-cultural bond. We were *acting* at being Southerners in those other years, rather than devoting ourselves wholeheartedly to the joyful pursuit of expressing our Southernness. We were taking a few hours off from being whatever we were, on a New Year's Day, and participating for old times' sake in a ritual that really didn't mean all that much to us. In actuality we were lawyers, writers, reporters, retired people, designers, teachers, fanciers of well-baked pecan pies; not necessarily Southerners.

This year it was different. The accents were more animated, more sincere. Nobody went out of his or her way to use any of the stereotypical expressions, such as "Yawl" or "Lord have mercy," but neither did anybody attempt, as many had on the other occasions, to hide his or her native mellowness behind the cold, curt cadences that we have all adopted to help us survive in the big city. Southerners who are away from their native land, you should know, have developed the facility for speaking in two languages. One, the language of the foreign land in which they find themselves; the other, the language of home. Black Southerners who live in the North and who do not spend much of their time in the white world use the language of home much more, but their white brothers, who are very much a diffuse minority in a place such as New York, have only infrequent opportunities to "speak Southern" to each other. When such an opportunity does arise, they seem to really enjoy it. There are few spectacles more devilishly perplexing to a sophisticated, knowledgeable Northern white than witnessing a meeting between a Southern white and a Southern black, perfect strangers to one another, and listening as they spring, almost immediately after discovering their shared origins, into a discussion of "home," or "down home," or sometimes just "back there," in a language that the Northerner can hardly begin to comprehend.

The Southern language was spoken almost exclusively at the New Year's Day party that year, and it was spoken unashamedly. Our Northern friends, whom we jokingly referred to as "observers," watched in fascination and sometimes joined in, to the degree that they were able. I noticed two of them sneaking Moon Pies into their coat pockets, no doubt so they could display them in an atmosphere of great hilarity at some later party attended solely by Yankees. "Got this at a party with some Southerners," they would no doubt say, and instead of making fun of us they would be according us a little—what? half-serious honor, respect?

One obvious reason for this respect was Jimmy Carter. A couple of months before, someone who was apparently a true Southerner had been elected as president of the United States, and in a few days would be sworn into office. A decade before, the election of a Southerner might have created a considerable stir (I do not count Lyndon Johnson as a Southerner, although from time to time he pretended to be one), but by 1976 and 1977 everything in American society, if it were to last in the public's memory past the end of the Ten O'Clock News, if it were to pay a profit on its promoters' investments, had to become a certified Super Media Event.

Thus, as Carter's ascendancy became a sure thing, the South became such an event. The media mills started cranking out new fantasies, fascinations, and foolishness, and the people who decide what will be fashionable started incorporating Southernness into their fall lines. Someone wrote a little book telling you how to talk Southern. A public relations woman advertised in *New York Magazine* that, for a fee, she could teach anyone to speak with a Southern accent. (A few years before, a bright, accomplished Atlanta black woman, a licensed elementary-school teacher, was turned down for a job in the New York City school system on the grounds that she sounded like a Southerner.)

In the summer of 1976, after the engineer-peanut farmer from Georgia was nominated at the Democratic convention in New York City, a fellow who runs some peanut stores there changed their names to "Carter's Nuts." A hotel in the heart of the Times Square retail raw-sex district changed its name from the Dixie to the Carter. Somebody wrote that grits grew on grit trees and a lot of people in the sophisticated North believed it.

When the Democratic party crowned Carter with the nomination, and the Rev. Martin Luther King, Sr. (known in Atlanta as Daddy King), started a relatively tame version of a Deep South black Baptist benediction, a lot of nice Northern white people couldn't understand it at all. Their television screens had never brought them anything like that. They really got confused when all the Democrats joined hands and started to sing "We Shall Overcome," the overcomees presumably being Gerald Ford and Robert Dole. The crowd scene that appeared on our television screens at the end was the ultimate moment in the game of Southern politics, a game that is played with such religious fervor that most of the Democrats actually taking part probably didn't realize they were profaning the anthem of a movement for which dozens of people had given their lives.

There they were, all of a sudden: blacks, whites, Little Amy, Miz Lillian, Coretta King, the triumphant candidate—and, in a shot from a slightly different angle, from a camera off to one side, George Wallace, the racist who lived by the sword. He leaned slightly forward, in the wheelchair that will be his home for the rest of his life, as he was being elevated to the platform. It was like the movie, "Nashville."

Was it all a farce, a tacky attempt at putting on a wing-ding of a Super Media Event—or did these people *believe* in what they were doing? It was true, wasn't it, that what brought them together was their *Southernness?* This man who was Martin Luther King's father—was that actually a *benediction* he was snatching out of the summer evening sky like sheets of lightning? And George Wallace and Mrs. King—didn't Wallace *hate* people like her?

I have a fine friend, a good white Northern lady, who

said she had to turn away from her television set and leave the room. She said she was physically sickened by the sight. The differences between the South and everything else, in that moment back in the summer of 1976, were simply too great for her.

Carter's nomination and subsequent election unquestionably played a major part in making the South a Super Media Event and in making the region generally more visible and more accessible to the nation as a whole. In doing so, it elevated the Southerner's—and especially the exiled Southerner's—feelings of pride for the place.

I know of few Southerners who, either during Carter's campaign or after his election, could express anything approaching complete trust in the man. Southerners, remember, have had much experience, most of it painful, with politicians who claim to be champions of the "little people." They also have had plenty of experience with well-to-do people who make a big public thing out of their religiosity, who go about promising that they will never tell lies and who fly around in airplanes owned by banks. Hypocrisy ranks right alongside RCs and Moon Pies as a staple in the lives of Southern movers and shakers.

But neither do I know of any ordinary Southerner who would deny that Carter's election helped build or restore his or her pride in the South. It was as if the South, in producing a man like Carter—quite imperfect, to be sure, but nevertheless possessing a certain degree of honesty, intelligence, style and charisma, a sort of white Martin Luther King, in fact (although that may be stretching it a bit)—had proved it was just as good as the rest of the country. Maybe better, when one considers the political creatures that have issued forth from other regions: Nixon, Nelson Rockefeller, many of the strange breed from Penn-

sylvania and Maryland, and, now that the details are beginning to be filled in, the Kennedys.

For years the white South had been told, particularly
by what was widely touted as an enlightened, sophisticated, liberal North, what a terrible place it was. Some of
its own sons and daughters—not many, to be sure, but
enough—had told the South, as well, of its transgressions.
And to an alarming extent the critics were correct. The
South had a great deal to rightly feel guilty about.

There was the region's awful record of producing, putting into office, and keeping there in perpetuity political
travesties, many of whom disguised themselves with the
lambs' skins of populists, but who ended by fleecing the
public. And then the later, slightly less crude politicians of
the sort of Wallace, the Longs, Stennis, Eastland, Ross
Barnett, the Talmadges, who treated the electorate with
similar contempt.

And there was the feeling, and often the substance, of
degeneracy in the Southland, a Faulknerian decay that was
so all-encompassing that the election of rotten politicians
was a totally predictable side effect. And there was, of
course, at the base of it all, the indisputable racism of the
white South. *Slavery* had been practiced there—indeed,
more than practiced—rationalized there, loved there,
fought for there. Modern-day white Southerners would
say, on those infrequent occasions when the subject was
raised, that they did not believe they were accountable for
the sins of their grandfathers. But I know few who would
not admit, in the darkest and most secret chambers of
their souls, and perhaps best after an evening of bourbon
in some summer-evening Atlanta backyard, that they *were*
accountable; that they *did* share some of the blame; that
they *did* bear the burden throughout their lives; and that
they knew of no effective way to relieve themselves of that
burden. That there was no expiation for this sin possible
in their lifetimes. The most they could hope for was that

the anguished stain would somehow be less visible in their offspring.

Much, certainly most, of this guilt was exaggerated and inflated, as guilt often is. It resulted, perhaps, from the white Southerner's looking around and seeing the result of so much discrimination, knowing it wasn't the work of the black people, and concluding that, therefore, it must be his doings. It helped that the Northern-based press always came to the same conclusion. But in order for the guilt to be lasting and effective, it had to be based on more than just that. Few white Southerners of whatever station found themselves unable to provide that small but essential foundation. For each of them—us—had participated in some form of racism, even if only in our minds: had used the word *nigger,* which we ourselves hated so much, if only in some cruel barroom jest; knew that our world just might be severely shaken up, if not collapsed outright, no matter how liberal we might be, if One Married Our Sister. Each of us had guilt for our own deeds and for those of our grandfathers. I was adopted and have no idea in the world who my grandfather was—even, strictly speaking, what shade of pink or tan his flesh was—but I have the guilt nevertheless. It is, and has been, a major factor in my life and in the lives of my fellow white Southerners. It is, and has been, an essential part of being a white Southerner, as basic as hog jowls and black-eyed peas on New Year's Day.

Now, when I looked around the gathering of Southerners in the Brooklyn brownstone, I thought I detected less of that guilt over being Southern. Not only were the accents easier to hear, but the food was being attacked more violently than in earlier years. The long, drawn-out, humorous Southern-type stories seemed to be more abundant that day, and the people stayed on well into the evening telling them. Few talked directly of Carter, but several spoke of friends and acquaintances who soon would be moving to Washington to take up jobs in the new administration. And, out of the corner of my eye, I detected what I was pretty sure were looks of jealousy on the faces of the Northern observers. It may have been bewilderment at hearing so many people speak Southern, of course. It may have been confusion over seeing black and white Southerners, who were, after all, supposed to be bitter enemies, embracing each other at the threshold and enjoying the same sorts of "soul" cooking that formerly had been associated in the Northerners' minds with blacks alone. It may, too, have been disgust at the sight of so much Southernism. (Like Texans, we *can* be a bit overpowering at times.)

I suspect it was a mixture of jealousy and confusion that crept across the Northerners' faces. Jealousy because there is little in the North to compare with a Southerner's feeling of love for the South, and it must be wrenching to watch a group of people who are happy about their homeland. Ask a Southerner to name the things that he or she is, and it is quite likely that high on the list, up there around "man," or "woman," or "data programmer," or "plumber," will be the term, "Southerner." Few Northerners, I think, except for those from crannies of New England where some geographical pride still exists, and a few remaining hard-apple-core New York City–lovers, would think to list the part of the country they were from.

There is confusion because Northerners as well as Southerners have been misled about the region and its people. Some Northerners seem to have assumed that Southerners are, by definition, little better than baby-eaters. Since they stayed away from the South and saw few Southerners, black or white (except, on trips to Miami, for those operators of Georgia speed-trap towns who very well *might* have been baby-eaters), the assumption was of little significance until recently. It really didn't matter all that much what Northerners thought of Southerners. Now, however, partly because of Carter's election, the energy crisis, and the "Sunbelt" boom—but really because the South has become a more important factor in all aspects of the nation's life—non-Southerners are being *forced* to confront the idea of the South and Southerners. And the more they hear and see about the place, the more they must alter their stereotyped picture of it. Now the South must be counted as part of any national assessment, whether non-Southerners like it or not. And so it is not surprising that a non-Southerner gets a bit confused.

The Southerners, on that New Year's Day, seemed to be not only aware of that rather unusual shift in events, but also to be taking advantage of it. It was with something approaching smugness that a few of us paraded our Southernness before both the Northern observers and each other. "No, Marvin," I heard myself saying in a voice far louder than necessary to a perfectly innocent friend from Leonia, New Jersey, "you don't cut a Moon Pie with a knife." All he had been doing was looking quizzically at the concoction.

There were some of us, of course, who did not take part in all this rudeness; freedom comes not only slowly, but also in different stages, in different degrees, and at different times to different people. The black Southerners, who had declared their liberation some years before, were more polite and didn't engage in the exercise at all.

It has become possible now, finally, for those of us who are from the South to make comparisons with the North and to make them out loud, to challenge the myths that held that the North was somehow better, somehow *nicer* than the South. It is becoming common knowledge that these myths are no longer acceptable. And who should know better how unacceptable they are than exiled Southerners? Black and white, rich and poor, smart and dumb, for a variety of reasons we had left the Southland years before and come to this cold Northern place to live, some of us claiming it would be for a short while, some swearing it would be forever. In my case it had been thirteen and one-half years since we had left Atlanta and come to the place that even then, and with greater justification, people were calling the Big Apple.

Whatever the reasons we gave for leaving, it is pretty certain we all felt there was something here in the North we needed that couldn't be obtained in the South. On that cold, damp New Year's Day in 1977, it seemed fairly clear that at least those of us who were wolfing down the hog jowls and black-eyed peas had learned an additional lesson: that there is something you can only get in the South. It had taken us a long time to come to that realization.

A young woman stood with her back to the fireplace. She had finished her obligatory RC and now was attempting to keep her cornbread from crumbling into her glass of white wine. Her voice was warm and soft and Georgian.

"You know," she said, "I've always been proud of being a Southerner. A lot of times Northerners have tried to make me feel guilty about being from the South, and sometimes they succeeded. But it's different now. I'm not guilty any more. I'm really prouder than ever of the South. We've got something going for us there that these people up here don't have; never heard of. It's so *cold* up here."

2

Some definitions
before leaving

The South. There is, of course, nothing approaching universal agreement about what constitutes the South. There have been attempts, though, at putting the place into one or more categories, and at least at defining its physical boundaries. The original Confederacy, certainly a collection of states that considered themselves Southern, was made up of Alabama, Arkansas, Florida, Georgia, Louisiana, Mississippi, North Carolina, South Carolina, Texas, Tennessee, and Virginia. An organization interested in the economic and other development of the region, the Southern Growth Policies Board, offers a fifteen-state South—the original Confederate eleven plus Kentucky, Maryland, Oklahoma, and West Virginia. The U.S. Bureau of the Census, being part of the government and therefore accustomed to doing things as it pleases,

15

adds two more political entities, Delaware and the District of Columbia.

That would seem to be enough definitions to choose from. But Southerners have added, from time to time, the state of Missouri to the list. And what of Southern Illinois? Surely if meanness and racism are Southern characteristics, as some think, downstate Illinois would qualify. And how to classify Louisville, a city that is as Southern as, say, Knoxville, but that for some reason denies it? A standard collegiate dictionary manages, perhaps wisely, to avoid naming any states at all when called upon to define *the South*. The original Mason-Dixon line might serve at least as a northernmost boundary, but nobody seems to remember where it is. And someone once suggested that the South was where substantial numbers of mules still were maintained.

Others would say that the South is anywhere below the line where restaurants will bring you grits in the morning (and that the *Deep* South is where they bring the grits without asking or being asked). But this definition excludes those portions of Tennessee where many citizens consider the day not properly started unless they are confronted with, not a tiny volcano of grits, its crater a megacaloric pool of molten butter, but a saucer of pale flour gravy and a plate of biscuits to dredge through it.

The South also exists in the North. The Bedford-Stuyvesant ghetto of Brooklyn has a population the size of Fort Worth's or Toledo's, and an enormous number of those people are from the South. Some of them buy their greens and hogmeat from a place called the North Carolina Country Store, which operates its own small-scale truck line to bring the delicacies of home to the exiled Southerners. Much of the lives of Bed-Stuy's residents, from the inflections of their voices to the passion of their religion, follows Southern patterns; it is almost as if they think of themselves as only *temporary* Northerners. And maybe they are, for thousands of them commute back "down home" every third or fourth weekend, maintaining their ties with the region of their birth. Many would stay there permanently if they had decent jobs there.

Not all Southern exiles are black. The Uptown area of Chicago is an enclave of Southern whites, many of them poor. Cities such as Dayton, Cincinnati, and Columbus have substantial Southern populations, black *and* white. An unknown number of Appalachian whites work on the Detroit assembly lines and commute each weekend to the hollows of West Virginia and Kentucky where their families still live. And in any large city of the North, Midwest, or West, there are exiled white Southerners who are not particularly ghettoized, who exist largely independent of one another, meeting only when an accent is recognized in a telephone conversation or by a chance encounter, or when a bluegrass or country-music festival is held or, occasionally, at a hog-jowls-and-black-eyed-peas gathering on a damp New Year's Day.

So we end up with very little definition of "the South" at all. Perhaps, for the purposes of this journey, we should simply define it as that geographical region which practically everyone calls "the South"—Virginia, North and South Carolina, Georgia, Florida, Alabama, Mississippi, Louisiana, Tennessee, eastern and southern Kentucky— plus, whenever it suits our needs or theirs, those other areas that from time to time consider themselves part of the phenomenon—places such as eastern Texas, West Virginia, the District of Columbia, Arkansas, and, to a lesser extent, Oklahoma and Maryland.

The Southerner. Since we don't know what the South is, it might seem unlikely that we could define the Southerner. Maybe, maybe not.

Many, perhaps most, of those who write or speak about

Southerners are speaking only of white Southerners. Some never think of blacks from the South as being "Southerners" at all. Those who are more perceptive and sensitive at least explain why they confine the definition to whites. John Shelton Reed, a Chapel Hill sociologist and one of the very few members of his trade who has a sense of humor and can write clearly, says almost apologetically in his book, *The Enduring South,* that he is using the white-only definition because it is "common usage." He adds: "It is symptomatic of Negroes' exclusion from much of Southern life that they are typically excluded from the very category, 'Southerner.'"

Blacks *are* excluded, for it's usually white people who decide what is "common usage." I would wager that if anybody asked them, black people from or living in the South would respond that they think of themselves as Southerners. Maybe they don't use the term as frequently as whites. Maybe they are preoccupied—because the rest of society has for so long been preoccupied—with their being blacks first. But I have never seen or heard a black Southerner wince or groan or complain when I have referred to him or her as a "Southerner." Besides, black Southerners *are* Southerners. They are of and by and from and for the South at least as much as their white brethren, and they have repeatedly demonstrated, particularly in the years since 1960, when the best-known wave of sit-ins started in Greensboro, North Carolina, their love for and faith in the region.

We could define Southerners as being all the residents of those states arbitrarily chosen as constituents of *"the South."* But that seems like something of a cop-out. Is a retired New York City detective who lives in a South Florida condominium built on land stolen from the Everglades by some sleazy realtor a Southerner by any stretch of the imagination? Are West Virginia mountain people Southerners or mountain people? Are former Nazis now living in Huntsville, Alabama, Southerners? Are the people who run Houston anything at all?

Quite a few intelligent observers of the region prefer to think of Southerners as an ethnic group, as distinct in their traits, customs, language, and rituals as the Jews of Flatbush, the Irish of Boston, the Poles of Chicago, the Cubans of Miami, or the German-Americans of Frankenmuth, Michigan. This approach is an attractive one; when it is employed, the Southerner's geographical location ceases to be of over-riding importance. Space is automatically created in the definition for the exiles currently living in the cold North and for those who go to California (temporarily, of course, but how many of them ever come back?) to encourage the sun to scramble their brains a bit.

Perhaps the best definition is the one that, like the one for the South, squirms furthest away from anything concrete: if you feel like a Southerner and say you're a Southerner, then you're obviously a Southerner. After all, who'd want to lie about something like that? (Until recently, it was unthinkable that anyone other than the most vulgar practical joker would want to falsely claim Southernhood. But it's getting fashionable now to be Southern. This may eventually create a problem. Some people used to go to England for short times, as the political-scientist–politician–Nixon-strategist, Daniel P. Moynihan, did, and come back with British accents and mannerisms which they retained their whole lives. Ten years from now, will proper Bostonians and Newporters take the Southern Crescent to Atlanta for a few days and return to their clubs saying ''Yawl'' and advising their friends at the conclusion of dinner parties on Beacon Hill and along Bellevue Avenue to "Drive real careful, now, and come back real soon, you hear?'')

The North. This, unfortunately, will be at least as amorphous as the definition of the South. Ordinarily it will mean not just the states in the Northeastern section of the United States but also the entire non-South—even such patently non-Northern places as Colorado and California. For, just as many non-Southerners fail to notice the subtle and not-so-subtle distinctions among the components that go into the South, and thus lump it all together into "the South," by the same token, many Southerners say "the North" when they mean to say "the rest of the country." It is the non-Southern country that is reflected most on the evening television news, in the deliberations of Congress and the rulings of the Supreme Court, in the dirty-little-boy chatter of the Carson show. To a Southerner, "the North" takes in everything from Mary Tyler Moore to the Pentagon, to the crime and municipal bumbling of the Big Apple, to even poor old Walter Cronkite.

This latter institution demonstrated, during the 1976 Democratic convention, the sort of ignorance that even intelligent and sensitive Northerners have always shown about the South—a sort of ignorance that says, "If it happened in the South it isn't very important." Cronkite was interviewing Lillian Carter. Miz Lillian was trying to say something of importance, and Cronkite was patronizing her, presumably in accordance with his role as a representative of a society that rarely acknowledges that women, and especially older women, have anything important to say.

Miz Lillian was talking about populism. Specifically, she was talking about Tom Watson, a former Congressman and Senator and Georgia's premier populist until his death in 1922. Watson was a key figure in the entire populist movement as well as a Grade-A racist; his history helps explain the rise and success of such presumably diverse modern figures as Jimmy Carter and George Wallace.

"You know Tom Watson?" Miz Lillian half said, half asked, in the process of making her point.

"The postmaster general?"replied Cronkite, hesitantly. He apparently had no idea who Tom Watson was. Or perhaps it was just that the little plastic thing in his ear was telling him to get ready for a commercial, and he was plunged into temporary forgetfulness.

To compound all the confusion over the region, "the North" frequently will be used to mean New York City, and vice-versa. This will undoubtedly seem to some, especially those who live in Northern but demonstrably non-New-York-City-like places such as Mystic, Connecticut; Stowe, Vermont; and Jim Thorpe, Pennsylvania, to be an awful error, if not an indictable offense. I recognize the dangers in this usage, and I apologize in advance for my foolishness. New York City is, in many ways, the logical end result of so much that is going on in the non-South. I mean it to serve here as the symbol of what much of the nation, but not yet all of the South, has become, or will become if we're not careful.

Warmth. As used here, the term will swing back and forth between two of its meanings. It will refer to the physical warmth of a place (in this case, the South, which, in general, has a comfortably higher temperature than other regions), and it will mean emotional warmth, a sensation that I believe also exists in inordinate degree in the Southland. The two sorts of warmth often blend into one in the South. I suspect I am not alone among Southerners exiled to the North, even those of us who have learned to love the Northern winter forests, silent and lovely in their deep February snows, when I say that in the winter time we think especially of the South and of its special warmth. We know that before winter is half over in the North, the people who remain in our homeland, in the region of warmth, are already starting to think about another spring.

3

The journey begins

Warmth was very much on my mind when I left New York that January morning and headed south. It had been snowing in New York, but the dogs and trucks and salt spreaders had been out turning it brown and nasty. The salt stained your boots white and took away much of the beauty of the snow; the whole effect was one of cold ugliness. Many people in New York hate the winter's snows because they see only this side of it. I drove without stopping, except for toll booths, until I got around Washington on the deadly frantic 495.

It had snowed in Virginia and North Carolina, too, but there the snow was still white and lovely. The day before, the temperature had risen above freezing and the snow had started to melt. At night it had frozen hard again, and the result was a fine, smooth crust that was no fun to walk on, but that made the countryside look incredibly beautiful. It was like a white-surfaced mirror. The sun was out, and the crust reflected its light on fields and hills of faultless white, like the glint of sunlight on a river as seen from an airplane high above. All that sunlight made things warmer, too, or at least it gave the impression of warmth. It was still quite cold, but not as cold as the North.

Off to the west were the mountains, the Blue Ridge and the mountain named Massanutten, and then the Shenandoah Valley, and the Shenandoah Mountains, the Alleghenies, all part of the Appalachians, mountains that march all the way from Alabama into the sea at Nova Scotia but mountains which I will always think of as products of the Southland. The mountains were, on this day, blue: shades and densities of blue that varied in very subtle ways, overlapping each other, lumping mightily across the horizon, turning whichever way they wanted to, taking the shapes they damn well pleased. It is easy to anthropomorphize mountains. They say Come see me, come walk me, come climb me, and from a distance they look like the most graceful and accommodating creatures on God's earth. But you know that they can be dangerous, too.

I was well off the hated interstates now. The countryside was fine-looking, and would have been fine-looking even without the snow. The farms here were small and getting along in years, but they were not run down; the people who owned and lived on them believed in work. The car passed over creeks and streams that were frozen except for patches where the ice was so thin you could see the clear, cold water rushing past underneath. It would be good to drink, you thought, but you knew that these days there was, as likely as not, a plastics or pesticide plant upstream that dumps some horrible cancerous poison in the water.

I passed a cemetery of the newer kind that discourages the placement of large, upright headstones. Every dozen yards or so a spray of plastic flowers grew out of the snow. In one place a large blanket of flowers, not plastic, covered a new grave. The plastic flowers nearby contrasted harshly with the white snow, but the real ones did not look so out of place.

Not far past the graveyard came Charlottesville, and the plastic started for real. In one block I passed a Pizza Hut, a Long John Silver's Seafood Shoppe, a Lord Hardwicke Inn, a Shakey's Pizza Parlor, a Hardee's Charco-Broiled Hamburgers, an Arby's Roast Beef Sandwich Is Delicious, and a Prime Rib. There were several others, but I failed to get their names. I sighed a sigh of resignation, of disappointment, as I always do when I see plastic in the South.

This was not, of course, the first time I had been back to the South since I had traveled north thirteen and one-half years before. But it was the first time I had returned for the express purpose of studying the South. "Studying" sounds a bit more high-falutin than it should; it was the first time I had ever had a financially supportable excuse for traveling through the region and writing down notes about what I saw and heard and smelled and felt. For that I am indebted to *The Charlotte Observer*, which is quite likely the best newspaper in the South. Dave Lawrence, the newspaper's editor, commissioned me to write a series of twenty-six articles, appearing once a Monday for half a year, on the South. The series was called "Southern Journey" and is the basis for this book.

Each of those times I had returned to the South, working on stories or visiting or, during flush periods, going there on vacations, I had been "paying attention to the place," of course. A Southerner rarely loses all touch with the South. I don't know of many non-Southerners who feel that way about the regions of their birth, although I suspect that people from the Northwest coast are in the same category.

"Paying attention to the place" has always meant being aware of the condition of the physical environment. It is always reassuring, when you're heading south down the highways, to see that the rivers and streams and mountains are still there; that they haven't been diverted or dried up or flattened by the dispassionate hand of some real estate developer or some paper-shuffler at the Corps of Engineers.

And you pay attention to the development that has occurred since you last visited. You know there has been some, because that is the way of the South these days. It is growing; few are raising their voices against *that*. What you hope is that the development that has occurred will, somehow, against all the odds, turn out to be *attractive,* good development that will enhance the region rather than scar it. You have left so many of those scars behind you on the interstate gutter down from New York to Baltimore.

But the scars are everywhere. The Pizza-Hut-Long-John-Arby-Charco-Delicious-Rib-Burger-HoJo-Ramada-7-11-Big-Mac-K-Mart-King-Burger plastic is upon us. The scars grow first along the interstate cloverleaves. And when the cloverleaves are full, the junk spills out along the Frontage Roads that run parallel to the interstate and on into the highways that enter the sides of towns that are more well-to-do. Often when you are driving all the way through a city on an interstate, you will see no plastic at all on the poorer side. That is just one of the differences between the poor and non-poor sides of towns, between white people and black people, between poor whites and middle-income whites.

I call all this the enfranchisement of America. By this I mean neither the freeing of the nation from slavery or the delivery to it of the right to vote. I mean that America in

general, and much of the South in particular, have become overridden with franchise operations—chain outfits,
not responsible to the communities in which they operate,
neither aware of nor interested in the subtle variations in
taste and character from region to region, state to state,
that are what make America interesting. The franchises
stand there on the cloverleaves and on the Frontage
Roads on the "better" sides of town, looking just like all
the others in their chain, providing the same dull, predictable, low levels of service, quality, and taste.

None of this is necessarily bad in every sense. Critics of
the fast-food business have subjected Big Macs and Quarter-Pounders to intensive analysis and have determined
that, while they may widely be called junk food, they're
perfectly nutritious. That is a beneficial side to the dullness and predictability. In theory these franchise operations probably constitute the only efficient way to serve
the needs of large, mobile populations of people who get
most of their information from television, who routinely
send to the top of the best-seller list book versions of the
movies they have seen and quick volumes written by medical hustlers, who fix dinners utilizing recipes that appear
in the advertisements of women's magazines, who would
sooner die than miss a professional football game, whose
main desire in life is no longer achieving happiness for
themselves but the still worthy idea of getting for their
children better educations than they themselves had, who
have lost the ability to walk and who now are hopelessly
addicted to the automobile. I do not condemn these people. They are only doing what they have been told by the
media that they must do. It is comforting to them, perhaps, that the plastic places are interchangeable. No one
K-Mart offers a higher quality of blue jeans than another;
no single Burger King turns out blander mixtures than
another. It is the logical result of what used to be called
the Howard Johnson's Syndrome: you may not like what

they serve; you may make endless fun of the blurbs on the menu; But By God At Least You Know What You're Getting In A Howard Johnson's. You won't get anything exciting, but neither will you get diarrhea.

So how does all this apply to the South? In a couple of ways. The South is more prone to the disease of enfranchisement, because the South is rapidly becoming a suburban region. It has few large cities; those that it does have did most of their growing after the development of the massive American trend toward suburban living. So what has been built in the central cities of the South, often on land expropriated from poor whites and blacks, has been modeled after the Frontage Road mentality of the suburbs. The older cities of the North—Boston, Philadelphia, Baltimore, New York—did their developing much earlier, and different patterns were formed. It is debatable whether those patterns are better or worse than suburbia's, but at least in the older cities you can get a decent slice of pizza and really good Chinese food and occasionally a delightful ferry-boat-ride or stroll through an urban park, if you know where to look.

The South's susceptibility to enfranchisement is also heightened by the fact that the region is almost totally dependent on the automobile for personal transportation. Mass transit barely exists in the South. Mass *rapid* transit is limited to a system being built in Atlanta and one in operation in Washington. Most Southerners who get around feel, with some justification, that they must get around in an automobile, and the franchise operations function parasitically off the automobile.

There is another way in which the enfranchisement movement affects the South. Southerners, along with some Westerners and a few New Englanders, are the last Americans who are cantankerous. They are the last ones with independence, the last ones who find it possible to express what many others only feel: their great contempt for the bureaucracies and other institutions that would hold them down and squeeze them into dumb submission. Enfranchisement knows that such people exist, and sets up devices for giving the *illusion* that such people are being accommodated, but in the long run the eccentrics lose. They are told by a hamburger chain that they can "have it your way," but somehow the end product always tastes the same. There is something in the process of enfranchisement that makes an onion taste less like an onion, a pickle taste less like a pickle. The giant shopping center discount store promises the citizen in search of a pair of gloves or socks that "one size fits all," but of course it doesn't. The store knows the sucker probably won't bring the merchandise back if it doesn't fit, but just in case he does there is an exchange procedure designed to wear him down and discourage him into absorbing the loss. The gloves weren't going to last very long, anyway.

All this, I think, runs counter to the traits and characteristics of the South. Southerners pride themselves on their individualism (although many of them are not very tolerant of it in others), and enfranchisement plunges a knife into the very heart of individualism. It reduces us all to quiet, patient ciphers who stand in lines without complaint and who accept what is offered without question. It is one of the many steps the nation has taken in recent years to reduce its citizens to numbers.

The motel in Charlottesville was part of a large chain of places that claimed to be of the "budget" variety. I started filling out the room-registration form and noticed that there was a space for my driver's license number. Not the car's license-plate number, which motels have always demanded, but my *driver's license* number. I asked why.

The clerk stiffened. He realized, quickly, as people in such jobs do, that he was dealing with a trouble-maker, one of those customers who asked why rules were made. His reply was a bit curt. "The company that insures us requires it," he said. The insurance company: the ultimate franchise operation.

"But why my driver's license number?" I asked.

"I can see you're not from Virginia," he said, "or you'd understand." He sounded as if he were explaining something to a slightly retarded child. "In Virginia, your driver's license number is your Social Security number."

"But why do you—or the insurance company—need my Social Security number?"

"It's not *my* rule," he said. "It's the company's rule, and the insurance company's rule."

"Well, then," I said, "I guess it's *my* rule not to stay in places that need my Social Security number." I tore the registration form in half.

"You can't tear that up," said the clerk. His superior, slightly snotty attitude was gone now; he became genuinely upset at the sight of my tearing the form.

"The form's got a *number* on it," he said. "Only I can void it. It'll mess up all the books at the company." I tore it into even smaller pieces and walked out and drove to an old-fashioned motel that wanted only my money and my license-plate number.

In Charlottesville that night, at the home of an old friend, we sat around the fireplace and drank and talked about how ancient we had all gotten since last time, and we wasted not five minutes in getting to the subject of Jimmy Carter. The gathering was mostly faculty from the University of Virginia: the editor of a fine literary quarterly, a member of a newspaper family who had deserted the presses for the groves, and a distinguished historian.

"I'm not sure," said the former newspaperman, "that I don't rate Carter as a power broker without ideology."

Everybody seemed to agree with this. Carter had been in office for only a few days, but already we were figuring him out.

"But what a symbol for the South," said the historian. "Just think of the access this is giving to so many people who didn't have access before." It was true. Even I, who trusted Jimmy Carter no more than I trusted Lester Maddox (perhaps less, because Carter had said he would never lie to me), felt now that I had some sort of a stake in the future of the nation that I hadn't had before. And that feeling came strictly as a result of the election of someone to office who was part of the same section of the nation of which I was part.

I stayed away from the plastic from Charlottesville to Raleigh. The highway was just a thin red line on the map, not a heavy blue interstate or a thick red divided roadway. It curved a lot the way old highways did before government started taking the power of eminent domain seriously, and it climbed up and down a lot of hills the way roads did before we learned to blast straight through anything that got into our way. But it was a real highway, one that showed you the character of the country, one where every crossroads could be, if you wanted, a "rest area," where every old-fashioned grocery store could be a "service area," and where everything was a "scenic area."

The rivers and streams meant something here, and most of them were marked. Often, on the interstates, you can cross a truly wide and obviously important body of water and there will be no sign identifying it. Here, on the secondary roads, the old bridge signs remain. I crossed the Hardware River, and then its beneficiary, the James, a beautiful river that less than a hundred miles downstream has been turned into a poisonous sewer by the Allied Chemical Company.

A firm shockingly named Life Science Products Company, working for Allied, for seven years dumped an insoluble roach poison known as kepone into the river at Hopewell, Virginia. The poison has sickened the firm's workers and ruined the fishing industry in the lower James and its tributaries. Allied has paid out more than twenty million dollars because of the contamination (which you and I pay for every time we buy something made by Allied Chemical), and no one knows how or when or if the James River will be made safe again.

I crossed the Appomattox, and passed towns named Dillwyn and Sprouse's Corner and Barnes Junction. Somewhere along the way I saw a roadside place that looked as if it might have barbecue, and it in fact did. The red clay started at Clarksville, just above the huge reservoir that straddles the Virginia-North Carolina line. The edges of the lake were frozen and big, black birds with long crooked necks stood on the thin ice and tore at something embedded there. It was probably unusual in their experience to be dealing with ice. Their whole bodies convulsed with the pecking operation, as if it were a sexual act. Perhaps when you're totally responsible for rounding up your food every day as they are, it is.

In Raleigh I saw my cousin David, the cousin I was always closest to when we were kids, and I told him I planned to walk Crabtree Creek the next day. David didn't say anything about how cold it would be out hiking because he knew it was never too cold. He is a geologist who works for the Highway Department, and he spends much of his time in the out-of-doors.

"You're going to be surprised," he said. "Distances have closed, man. What we used to think was five or six miles up the creek from Lassiter's Mill to the highway, well, that isn't more than fifteen minutes now. It's amazing. We used to play down there and think it was the biggest place in the world. We thought it was the damn *frontier*. The distances have gotten shorter as we've gotten older."

David was right. The stretch of the creek that we loved so much, between Lassiter's Mill and the Durham Highway, had always seemed to us, when we were kids, to be endless. We loved the creek and the woods around it, and we went there at least once a week all year long. We canoed there in a boat one of the Lassiters had made out of a World War II fighter plane fuel tank and that he rented to us for sixty cents an hour. It had no stability and turned over frequently. We hiked there, and camped there, and one winter David sent away to L. L. Bean for some traps and we trapped there. That section of the creek was interminable wilderness for us. Now it was less than two miles long, and I think I could have walked it in half an hour if I hadn't stopped to explore and think and eat lunch.

I parked at the ruined mill site and walked past the "No Trespassing" signs to the beginning of the trail that ran along the south side of the creek. The mill was gone, and had been for years. I used to bring home cornmeal that I had watched being ground on its huge, slow wheel. I never really appreciated, until much later, after my parents had died, the taste of the cornbread Mother made, or the Alabama cornpone Daddy made by patting out the hot wet meal between his hands.

The dam was the same, with its sandy beach below and the quiet but fast-moving waters above. The old one-lane bridge was closed now; they had built a bypass around it a quarter of a mile downstream to take the shoppers out to North Hills, a suburb with a shopping center that used to be farmland and woods. The new bridge was totally without character; when you were on the bypass you hardly even noticed you were crossing Crabtree Creek.

The creek was about the same size as it had been thirty

years ago—maybe a hundred feet wide—and the same color, a somewhat unhealthy-looking brownish-green. We used to joke about how the level of the Crabtree and the stream it emptied into, the Neuse River, rose two feet at precisely 12:15 P.M. on Sundays because that was when everybody got home from church, visited the bathroom, and flushed the toilet. We were not far from wrong. We made fun, too, of the creek, even though we loved it, because it was so obviously no-account.

Now I'm not so sure. I suspect the water is a lot cleaner, and I know, because I have taken to sailing along the coast, that the Crabtree and the Neuse are quite valuable. They gather their waters across half the state of North Carolina and empty them into Pamlico Sound, a vast bay behind the Outer Banks that is rich in seafood and the nutrients that make more seafood, that cleanses the water and the air and provides recreation for hundreds of thousands of people. Back when David and I were kids we never thought about hundreds of thousands of people, and the only seafood we thought of when we thought of Crabtree Creek was catfish, which were widely believed to be so shameless that they would survive in any environment, no matter how filthy. It was because of Crabtree Creek, and my knowledge of the sewage that flowed into it, that I have never been able to eat catfish, which is considered by many Southerners to be a great delicacy.

The trail closely hugged the edge of the creek, threading through the fairly dense growth. Old trees, their deep roots undercut by the erosive action of the stream, leaned out over the water as if they had keeled over yesterday, but I remembered some of them from my youth; they had always been that way. You could feel spring coming, although it was January. It was a cloudy day, getting cloudier, with the temperature somewhere in the thirties. A more wintry day would be difficult to imagine. But there was just enough color in the moss and the thorns and vines to tell you that spring would come.

The trail ran very close, now, to a street that belonged to a subdivision. I remembered when they opened that subdivision, maybe thirty years before. They used twin auctioneers in frock coats and tall, Abe Lincoln–type hats to sell off the large lots. The twins stood in the back of a pickup truck and moved slowly down the streets, selling land. The contractor, who was the father of a friend of mine, gave free Coca-Colas to the whole crowd.

The subdivision, I saw now, had stayed pretty much the same. The houses, some of which had looked rakishly "modern" back when they were built, had aged nicely and seemed perfectly ordinary now. They, and the entire housing development, posed no threat at all to the creek. I didn't even see any paths down from the road.

Panther's Lair—that's what we used to call the pile of boulders that formed a natural cave. It was said that a panther lived in there at one time. One of David's older brothers, Glenn, slept in the cave one night to show that he wasn't scared. Across the creek there were wooded back yards of houses where before there had been all woods. A dog in one of the back yards barked at me, but it was desultory barking, as if the dog knew only a fool would respect territorial claims made all the way across a creek. The houses were widely spaced and well removed from the creek. It is against the law in Raleigh now to build a house on the flood plain, and Crabtree is a very old creek and thus has a wide flood plain.

There was remarkably little trash: a wine bottle here and there (the creek had always been attractive to the gentlemen of the road), a beer can or two. There were few signs that people used the trail. I crossed a frozen side stream by jumping over it. Years ago, we were greatly influenced by Tarzan movies and would swing across on vines. This was about where we trapped a mink. We got there in the morning and saw the creature, dead in the trap, its body frozen, terror in its eyes. I felt awful about it for years.

I came to a large cleared space. A line of tall power pylons cut through the woods on both sides of the creek and crossed it, and in the process the electrical monopoly had leveled the ground in a forty-yard-wide swath. It was red mud now, because the bastards had killed all the vegetation. My father used to lecture me on the depraved nature of railroads, one of which he had once worked for. Now, I think, the utilities have taken the railroads' place.

Across the creek, someone had built a little dock. In another yard there was an aluminum canoe. Someone had built a little platform on the bank, in the general shape of a pyramid, and on the top had put a seat, which was obviously for sitting and looking at the creek.

I passed a tree, a particularly large one, that leaned halfway out over the creek, and I realized that I knew it, just as I might know a human I passed on a sidewalk. There was no single, particular identifying characteristic; I simply knew the tree. I placed my hand on it as I went by, and I felt a warmth there.

There were the remains of a campfire, and not much farther on the hum started: the multi-lane highway between Raleigh and Durham, a beastly affair with cloverleaves and shopping centers and miles and miles of plastic and, always, a hum of traffic that became, if you got close enough to it, a roar. I turned and started back toward my own car.

When I was a child in Raleigh, I always thought of Crabtree Creek as *my* creek. It had no apparent owners. The trails ran alongside the water, and they were always considered public passageways, just as the ocean beachfront is. Occasionally someone who owned the land at an access point, such as down at the mill, would post "No Trespassing" signs, but nobody ever paid attention to them and nobody ever enforced them. It was *my* creek, but my ownership didn't infringe on anyone else's ownership of it. Now, thirty years later, I felt as if I still owned it.

It hadn't been sold, filled in, paved over, diverted, or ruined, as so many other features of the environment have been. In fact, the creek now was enjoying more protection than ever before. Perhaps there was some hope left.

4
Some more definitions

In 1941 a South Carolinian named W. J. Cash published a book that many feel is still the classic volume on the South. *The Mind of the South* remains as a basic text and reference work for serious scholars of the region. Cash started out as a teacher, then went to *The Charlotte News* as a reporter, editorial writer, and book reviewer. Shortly after the book was published he hanged himself, for reasons never completely explained, in a Mexico City hotel room.

His aim, as the name of the book implies, was to define the South—to explain its very mind. He announced immediately, in the first sentence, that the region was different from other places: "There exists among us by ordinary—both North and South—a profound conviction that the South is another land, sharply differentiated from the rest of the American nation, and exhibiting within itself a remarkable homogeneity." The place, wrote Cash, possessed in its formative years "a fairly definite mental pattern," a "complex of established relationships and habits of thought, sentiments, prejudices, standards and rules, and associations of ideas. . . ." The components of that mental pattern were many and varied. There was, in the South and in Southerners (Cash wrote primarily of the white Southerner) a "tendency toward unreality, toward romanticism, and, in intimate relation with that, toward hedonism."

That devotion to pleasure could be tricky. Southerners subscribed to a form of puritanism that outlawed almost all pleasures except "those of orgiastic religion and those of violence." But the early Southerner—and here Cash was talking of the white male—also had an inclination to sneak into the woods to play cards and drink whiskey, to force his sexual attentions on black women (having placed the white ones on unattainable pedestals), "to require secrecy and the guilty sense of sin as necessary conditions of the highest zest."

The physical world of the South was a prime ingredient in the region's mental pattern, with its near-constant growth cycle and its summer warmth that was capable of "blurring every outline and rendering every object vague and problematical." That physical world, wrote Cash, itself formed "a sort of cosmic conspiracy against reality in favor of romance." And, as proof of this, he offered a word-picture of the "dominant mood" of the Southland, its sunny afternoons and warm earth, its hazes and perfumes and moods—and then reminded the reader that the outgrowth of all this is "invariably a thunderstorm." That passage may well be one of the finest ever written about the physical world of the South, and it says a great deal about the region's emotional world as well.

The Southerner, Cash said, was brave, generous, courteous, loyal, intolerant, and violent, devoid of any capacity for rational analysis. The South's intellectual and esthetic culture was so superficial as to be "not a true culture at all." The Southerner was a great devotee of individualism, and yet he suppressed dissent in others, frequently with violence. Some eccentricity was tolerated, but when it touched "the great central nerve of slavery" the toleration disappeared. And "From the taboo on criticism of slavery, it was but an easy step to interpreting every criticism of the South on whatever score as disloyalty—to making such criticism so dangerous that none but a madman would risk it." All this brought the South to what Cash liked to call "the savage ideal": a situation in which "dissent and variety are completely suppressed and men become, in all their attitudes, professions, and actions, virtual replicas of one another."

At the bottom of it all, of course, was race. The white male could slip in every way it was possible to slip—into poverty, degeneracy, most forms of addiction, and probably a touch of bestiality—and still retain one bit of life-saving assurance: the knowledge that he remained superior to the black. The rules, which of course were written by the whites, *said* he was superior. It was the Southern way. It was, in Cash's mind and in the mind of many others before and after him, the most important single factor about the South, and the one that spread its influence into all other areas. Cash called it a "hypnotic Negro-fixation," the "ancient fixation on Negro."

More recently, others have added to Cash's comprehensive list of presumed Southern qualities. Not surprisingly, there are disagreements. Some examples might include these:

Southerners are more politically conservative than people elsewhere in the nation, and their politicians are more given to crudeness.

On the other hand, some would respond, the Southern ideal of political populism is the most revolutionary one since the war with England (although it's too bad it has never progressed from the ideal to the real). As for the crudeness of politicians, what of the late Nelson Rockefeller and Attica? Or the mayor of Philadelphia, several of the governors of Maryland, or Chicago's Daley?

There is less disagreement on another point: that Southern voters enjoy the game of politics more than anyone else.

Southerners have an innate wisdom that transcends book-learning.

Southerners are dumber than most other people. (H. L. Mencken, the sage of that temple of intellectual ferment, Baltimore, wrote of the South in a famous 1917 essay that "It would be impossible in all history to match so complete a drying-up of civilization.")

The South is rural. Its people are close to the soil, even if they're removed by several generations from the actual working of that soil.

The South is the next great industrial frontier.

The South is the next frontier of unionism.

Southern working people are distrustful of labor unions.

Southern textile mills are paternalistic in a good way.

Southern textile mills are trying to revive the institution of involuntary servitude.

Many Southern textile mill workers really don't want such Communist-inspired fringe benefits as decent pension plans, medical insurance, and job safety.

The South is religious. Not only are its people unashamed of their beliefs, they are proud of them.

The South suffers from a terminal case of religious hypocrisy.

The South is racist and anti-Semitic and will employ any degree of violence to preserve white supremacy.

The South is more fully integrated than the North, and relations between the races come as close as anything we now have to being a model for the nation.

Southerners are more respectful of the environment than others.

Southerners are more destructive of the environment than others.

The family is more important in Southern life. Personal relationships are primary—possibly even more so than money.

The Southern family is a snakepit of neuroses, and if you don't believe it then watch what happens when there's a death in the family and the survivors start dividing up the estate.

Manners are still important in the South.

Southerners have the manners of cowboys and the tastes of carnival geeks.

Southern living is carried on at a more relaxed pace.

Southerners may be more relaxed, but they're going to die young from all the pork, nitrates, and nitrites they consume.

And passion. Southerners are more passionately devoted to everything, from college football to stock-car racing, from women's rights to squirrel hunting. *Passion* is a word that comes up frequently in the South. There is a feeling, in much of the nation, that passion is a thing that goes into the flesh. In the South it goes further: It penetrates into the bone.

This passion can come out of a Southerner in a lot of ways: in the novels of a Faulkner, where it's churned together with a lot of alcohol and a fixation on depravity; in the lonely dark moans of a Thomas Wolfe; in the refusal by a dignified citizen of Montgomery to move from her seat on the bus; in the excitement of a tent revival on a vacant lot in Nashville or a political barbecue in south Georgia; in a teenager's first love in a spring soft with dogwood and cherry blossoms; or in the burning of a cross in a red-clay field on a Saturday night.

In January of 1977, three geographers from the University of North Carolina at Charlotte began a semester-long seminar course on the South. The three—James W. Clay, Douglas M. Orr, Jr., and Alfred W. Stuart—said they thought it was perfectly fitting that geographers should do such a thing, as opposed to historians or sociologists or anthropologists or psychologists. The South, after all, is a geographical entity. Clay, Orr, and Stuart had already done a fine job of proving that geographers could undertake a study of a single Southern state. Their book, *North Carolina Atlas: Portrait of a Changing Southern State,* published in 1975, is a jewel.

One of the semester's first sessions was devoted, as it should have been, to attempting to define the South. The fifteen or so students, all of whom were white, listed the elements they thought should go into such a definition. There was the matter of accent, said one. Not just accent, said someone else; it was more the way Southerners chose their words and terms. Someone mentioned the climate. Someone said it was the more relaxed life style.

None of the students mentioned race.

It is certain that if the question had been asked twenty years ago, or even ten years ago, someone—many people—would have named race, in one form or another, as part of the definition. The South *was* race. But nobody mentioned it now. The ancient fixation had gone somewhere. Could it have been eliminated from the minds of the people in that classroom? Or had it been repressed, suppressed? Or was it perhaps so obvious that everyone just *assumed* its presence? Or could it be that race had become less important to these young white Southerners than it might once have been—as it surely once had been?

II

Down the coast

5

A sweet sort of order

I stayed as close as possible to the coast as I headed south again from Brooklyn. Back in January, I had strained things a bit by detecting the imminent arrival of spring in the mosses and thorns, but in early April there was no question about it. The warmth was coming up from the South, and it drew me back. To make it even sweeter, I decided this time to stay by the coast.

The coast is where the sun comes from, where the moon comes from. They both emerge majestically and mysteriously from that enormous stretch of water that gives us life. Whenever I'm near it I wake up early and walk out to the beach and wait for the sun to force the water and the night sky apart. I love rivers, too, but I guess what I like most about them is the future that they hold, the fact that they broaden and marry and converge and become more important, even the tinier ones, as they approach the coast and enter the great estuaries.

It is especially important to stay away from the interstates when you're going down the East Coast. If you're heading into the American West, or across Texas, or through Kansas, interstates can be helpful. They can take you through the long, straight stretches in relative safety and speed and even with a little beauty. On the East Coast, they are little more than expensive traffic jams, perpetual rush hours, dominated by huge trucks, some driven by tailgating dopeheads, and by frantic urban motorists who don't know how to drive properly. The scenery is awful. The highways form a vast interstate sewer.

Such highways, like fast-food eating joints, are useful in emergencies. But under ordinary conditions, time spent on an interstate is time lost from your life; it simply vanishes from your allotted time on earth. And time spent on some such highways—notably the New Jersey, Pennsylvania, Ohio, and Richmond-Petersburg Turnpikes—is in an even worse category, being actually *subtracted* from your life. But time spent on secondary and back roads, especially those around the coast and the mountains, along with time spent on ferry boats, is time added to your life span. It enriches and refreshes and educates you. It is like time spent fishing for trout.

I took the hour-long ferry from the bottom of New Jersey to the top of Delaware. Not only is the ferry an attractive alternative to such depravities as the New Jersey Turnpike and Wilmington, Delaware, it also serves as an effective divider between the Northern and Southern cultures. When you drive onto the ferry at Cape May, you are leaving what is quite likely the worst state in the nation: the one that does the least to protect the environment or its citizens against harm in the name of industrial "growth." And when you drive off at Lewes, on the other side of Delaware Bay, you can detect the beginnings of the

South. The pace is slower, the people a little friendlier, the spaces a little more open.

Maryland is but thirty miles down the twisting roads, and not far beyond is Virginia. Some people say the South starts at the Virginia line; others can argue convincingly that Maryland is as Southern as most places. I stopped at a yard sale in Parksley, Virginia, and asked Linda Wessells, who was running it, whether she were a Southerner.

"I guess I am," she said.

Why?

"I just like the South better," she added. "I *could* be either one, I guess. Maryland's just a few miles up the road."

It was the second of April, a good time to travel the coast roads because it is the off-season and you can afford to stay at the beachfront motels. The people who run those places, who may be perfectly nice folks later in the season when the "No Vacancy" signs go up, are even nicer now. They have plenty of rooms to rent; they seem to think of the early-spring traveler as a harbinger of the customers yet to come; and they also seem to know that the off-season visitor must have a particular feeling for the beach or he wouldn't have gone out of his way to come here. The Ferris wheels are just stationary skeletons in early April; most of the ocean-front restaurants are closed; it is far too cold to swim. The visitor who comes now must come out of an attachment to the beach that is not shared by the public at large. It *is* shared, I think, by the innkeepers themselves.

The clerk on the first night, in Virginia Beach, spoke with a Southern accent but said he had been born and raised in New York City. "I've adapted to it," he said. He had been in the military, and that had brought him, like many others, to the Tidewater area. Norfolk and its sur-

rounding geographical area are so heavy with the uni-
formed products of Congress's pork-barrel system that the
land must be in constant danger of sinking into the sea.

The man looked a little strange: He had a cigar jammed
into his face the way a New Yorker does it—like a wise-ass
detective on a television series—and he had the look of a
New Yorker in his eyes; but he sounded like a Southerner.
He had *partially* adapted.

I paid him extra for an ocean-front room, moved my
luggage in, opened the door to the little patio, got a can of
beer from the cooler, and stood there, gazing at the beach.

In two nights the moon would be full; this night it had
risen behind wispy pearl clouds and its light shone
through from time to time as breaks occurred in the
swiftly-moving clouds. The water and the sky were both
slightly different shades of what the bottlers of fountain-
pen ink used to call Midnight Blue: the water a deeper,
denser color, the sky a little lighter than that but not very
much—you could hardly make out the horizon that sepa-
rated the two vast bodies. And moving across the lower
half, a widening and narrowing and disappearing line
that was the surf, creamy white, the lightest color of them
all. I stood and stared at all this, and suddenly I realized
that I had the old feeling again.

I am not capable of properly defining it. It has something to do with the feeling of balminess all around you,
and it has a great deal to do with the slow, soft rush of
warm air from the south. It is a feeling I have gotten only
in the Southland, and when I have gotten it I have almost
always been at the beach. The low bushes planted in front
of the balcony rustled, and I felt the breeze's breath on my
arm—not hot, not really even warm, but a degree or two
warmer than the ordinary air, and coming always out of
the south. You feel it often when you are standing on a
beach and you can not help but let your mind wander to
thoughts of warmth; of islands much farther to the south,

of tropical things, of the skinny leaves of palms and the motions and noises they make in the wind. Of warmth, of a whole region of warmth.

There was a boardwalk about thirty yards from my patio, and quite a few people were using it, despite the fact that it was close to midnight. An older couple in evening dress walked by. Several bicyclists passed. Someone stopped to light a cigarette against the wind. A young couple walked across the upper beach and down the boardwalk to a set of steps and down it to the beach proper, where they disappeared into the darkness. Two young women walked south on the boardwalk, and they passed two young men walking north. About two seconds after they passed, the young men turned around, in the universal reaction, and looked at the young women's backsides. Off to the left there was a fishing pier in fairly good repair. Underneath it, among its strong wooden pilings, there were some other young people, passing around a lighted joint. Back on the boardwalk, kids shot past on skateboards.

The moon, too, was getting high now; it had shaken off the clouds and was moving unfettered across the sky. I walked toward the surf. From behind me, from somewhere on the developed part of the beach, I heard a deep bass sound, repeating itself; undoubtedly from some dancing place or bar. It was competing with the sound of the ocean, and it was losing. The sound of the ocean is something that, once heard, you never forget. It is a sound that brings back other feelings; brings back warmth.

It draws us back, those of us who are hooked on the Southern seacoast. It pulls us windbags who have just turned forty-two and who are worrying about dying, and it pulls preachers, perverts, pot-smokers, young lovers, fishermen, fisherwomen, old folks, skateboarders. And none of us can explain what it is all about. The young people who have just discovered it think they are the only ones who've ever stumbled on it. The forty-two-year-olds come hoping to try once again to figure it out. And the old people, who know better, have given up trying to understand it. They are just happy with the opportunity to see and hear and smell the beach again.

The next morning, as I left, there was a clean-washed, scrubbed feeling about the beach and the sky was a brilliant light blue. The wind had shifted to the northeast during the night.

It was Palm Sunday. I cut through eastern North Carolina, taking the bridge across Albemarle Sound. Spring had come, and there were blossoms and new green leaves and dogwood everywhere. I stopped to take a picture. A man drove up, stopped, got out, and asked me if I had any palm. I said I didn't.

"I just got to get some palm," he said. "The children need it for church." He looked genuinely worried. He thanked me anyway and drove off.

They were sitting on the front porch of a simple frame house on Highway 32 in the town of Acre, North Carolina. They were suspicious of me when I stopped the car, the way country people sometimes are, the way black people have learned to be, when a white stranger walks up.

The house was on a modest lot. Next door there was room for a garden. From inside the house I could hear the sounds of pans and utensils being shuffled around, and I could smell the greens that I knew were in a big pot on the stove, simmering with the hogfat. The young woman on the porch was fine-looking, with clear, rich brown skin, open-faced, smiling, friendly, unsuspicious. She wore a flowing, shapeless dress that looked cool and comfortable. The young man, her cousin, sat on the other side of the porch. He wore jeans and a plain shirt and sneakers. We got to talking about the South, and I asked them about their definitions of "Southerner."

"You live in the South all your life, you're a Southerner," said the young woman.

"I usually think of geographical regions," said the young man. "East of the Mississippi and south of Virginia is the South to me."

"I disagree," said the young woman. "I think it's the customs more than the geography."

It turned out that the young woman lived in Brooklyn, about three subway stops from me. She worked for the New York City Department of Health. This was her family home; she had come back to Acre for the Palm Sunday weekend. She didn't want me to write down her name because, as she put it, "Actually, I left the office a little early to come here. About a *day* early."

"I've lived in Brooklyn for about six years," she said, "but I still consider here my home. Because this is where my family is located. This is where my roots are." Alex Haley has contributed one of the proudest words of all to the vocabularies of black Americans.

"The pace here is much slower," she said. "I'm used to open spaces and the flowers and being free." I wondered if she talked that way in the big city.

Her mother once went to visit her for a week in Brooklyn, but she didn't like it and left after a few days. "It was too crowded for her," said the daughter. "Too many people. So now I come here as often as I can." When the weekends and vacations are over and the daughter leaves for the long ride back up to the North, she loads up the car with pork, eggs, corn, preserves, greens, and vegetables. She does not much like the North, but the money is better there. Even that, she said, may be an illusion. "You make more money up there," she said, "but living there takes it all away."

She was worried, she said, that "the South one day will be more like the North. People are returning here and bringing their bad habits back from the North. What I can't understand is this: a lot of the people in the North are from the South. How can you leave from here, go up there, make more money, and live worse there than you do here?"

The young woman abruptly stopped speaking. "I've been talking like there was no tomorrow," she said. "I've been talking a blue streak. When I'm home, I have a custom of speaking all the time. When I first went to Brooklyn, I couldn't keep quiet, and people looked at me strangely. Now I don't talk very much up there."

Her cousin had been quietly listening to her, and now he spoke. "I've been going to college in Durham for the past three years," he said. "And I think there's a big difference between here and *there*. Here, you feel free and you can go where you want to. You can be by yourself when you want to be. It's not that way in Durham. I don't think it's a difference between the North and the South, but a difference between places with a *lot* of people and places with *not many* people. And the air's a lot cleaner here."

The young woman broke in: "And the wild flowers and the trees," she said. She was beaming. "All these things just seem to have a sweet sort of order to them."

Nick Fokakis and Spiro Kefalas are, as their names suggest, Greek-Americans. But they speak with Southern accents. They run the Crystal Pier at Wrightsville Beach, North Carolina, not far from the city of Wilmington, and they are Southerners. Nick was born in Hattiesburg, Mississippi, and Spiro is from Wilmington.

The pier is a classic Southern fishing pier. On the landward end there are a few motel rooms. Then a ramp leads up to the pier itself, which widens, at about the high-tide mark, to become a combination restaurant-fishing tackle shop-pinball arcade. Beyond that the strong old wooden pier stretches out over the Atlantic. People go there night and day, and an amazing percentage of them catch fish. I knew the pier from earlier days. There was a large, wooden amusement center connected to its landward end that was called the Lumina. My mother used to talk of the days when a trolley took you down the beach to the Lumina. By my time, the native American trolley was virtually extinct, but the Lumina still stood, with its pinball games, a huge bowling alley, locker rooms, restaurants, dance hall, and general air of sensuality. I know of no place like it in America today. You can buy picture postcards of the Lumina now for several dollars. Someone has laminated them to slabs of wood and Nick Fokakis and Spiro Kefalas sell them in the restaurant.

I asked Nick my by-now standard question about defining the South.

"It's more of a feeling for people," he said. "I had never been up North before, and one time I visited some of my cousins in New York, and at first it was a *shock*. But later, when you get to know Northerners, they're warm and friendly. I guess it's the pressures of highly concentrated living. I think the South is developing the same pressures. Things like urban sprawl, and racial trouble. We're just beginning to get the problems of concentration: problems with water and sewer lines. Wrightsville Beach has a moratorium now on high buildings and new sewer connections. A lot of people want it to remain a 'family beach.'

"But it's a lot better here. You can get to the woods easier. Everything's green here. And in lots of ways the place is improving. We used to have a lot of trouble getting the stuff that goes into our Greek salads. We used to have to bring our *feta* cheese all the way back from New York. Now we get it in Wilmington."

I asked Nick about race. Things looked more peaceful now, I said. What did he think?

"We're getting a lot of coloreds who were raised here and went away and are coming back," he said. "They say they just can't take it any more up North. *We've* changed quite a bit, too. The attitude of the Southerners"—here he was employing the term to mean white Southerners—"has changed. There's more of a true feeling of change in the South than in the North. I think the Southerner understands the Negro better." (He pronounced the word that has caused so many problems "Nigra.") "I think the Southerner has a great sympathy for him, too. I think the whites understand now how bad off the blacks were. I know something about discrimination myself. I was looked upon as a stranger in Mississippi because I was Greek, even though I was born and raised there.

"I'll tell you something else, too: I think Carter'll make a big difference. I think the North was ready for a change. They knew that the South as a whole, symbolized by Carter, portrayed a new sort of morality that they in the North wanted."

I went out to the end of the pier for the sunrise the next morning, and there were a dozen or so fishers already at work, if it may be called that. Then I went back into the restaurant and asked Spiro Kefalas for some breakfast. It was easy to see that the major attraction at the Crystal Pier at that hour was the gentleman who was holding forth from a table in the middle of the room.

He was an older man, undoubtedly retired, and he was a storyteller of the classical Southern sort. Or maybe he was a windbag. At any rate, he talked nonstop, and his stories got more and more ambitious. Another man, a few years younger, sat at the table with him. He listened to every word, a permanent grin on his face. "Jesse," he would say, "you're some tale-teller." Both men wore base-ball-type caps of the sort in vogue among blue-collar and pseudo-blue-collar men.

"Why, when I was young and in good shape," Jesse was saying, "I could jump up in the air and clap my hands three times and click my heels three times before I landed on the ground again." The younger man shook his head slightly, as if to say that this was straining his capacity for belief, but that he was believing anyway.

Jesse moved on to politics for a while, then religion, and then he got on the case of a local gentleman who had a drinking problem and liked to shoot his rifle off the pier. He stayed away from race. He clearly considered all the room his stage, all of us breakfast-eaters his audience. Much of what has passed through the years as our Southern literature has come out of the mouths of people like Jesse in places like this fishing pier restaurant.

I could hear Jesse's voice aiming itself at me, bouncing off the back of my head. He was saying something about a yellow Volkswagen with "Newyawk" license plates. Since I have a beard, there was little doubt as to who the alien was. I knew that he, like a not-yet-professional night-club comedian, felt his act was incomplete as long as one member of his audience ignored him. I refused the bait; I ate my eggs and grits and stared out the window, which was coated with salt from the ocean air.

An elderly couple came in. The man was wearing a baseball-type cap. They sat down a couple of tables from Jesse and the younger man. The storyteller quickly discovered that they were retired visitors from the Midwest. Jesse neatly absorbed them into his act by talking about the cost of living.

"Fifty dollars," he said. "That's just beer money for a week now." The retired man said something in enthusiastic agreement and Jesse had him. It was gradually revealed, in the ensuing conversation, that Jesse was a retired Army colonel, and that he came to the pier almost every day to fish, but mostly to talk—to seek out and entrap and hold an audience just as he was doing this day. I began to feel almost sorry that I hadn't joined in.

A large stuffed fish was on the wall in front of me. There was a big thermometer with the phases of the moon written on it. Jesse finished a tale about a giant jellyfish, and the older couple and the younger man laughed loudly. Spiro Kefalas just smiled, probably because he had heard the story before. The younger man slapped Jesse on the back, softly and playfully. Respectfully. "Jesse," he said, "you do just about anything you want to. I wish I was just like you."

I moved south again out of Wilmington, going against the inward-bound morning traffic, which was all knotted up just as it is in a large city. I passed signs advertising coastal second-home developments, and occasionally I'd see the entranceway to such a tract. A fancy gate would be there, with an almost-tasteful billboard announcing the wonders of the planned community within. A road would lead from the main highway through the gate and back toward the development. But the road would be dirt, and it would go nowhere. The builders had been hit, thank goodness, by the mid-seventies recession and they had had to abandon their destructive projects.

The main road got narrower and more curved and less hectic, and then I was out of Wilmington's sphere of influence. I passed through a community whose only apparent central asset was a prefabricated garage and, in it, a combination ambulance-rescue vehicle with the word "Emergency" written backwards on its front, so that motorists could read it in their rear-view mirrors. The vehicle had been polished to within an inch of its life, and you could tell that the community was proud of it.

The South Carolina welcome center at the border was immaculate, almost too neat and clean to be comprehended by someone who lives in the Northeast, where governmental facilities are generally filthy and reflect the contempt that the governments have for their workers and that the workers have for the public and for their jobs. There were neat little garbage cans with neat little plastic liners, and not a speck of trash or garbage on the ground; shaded picnic spots; telephone booths that worked; and great quantities of vacation literature. It was, of course, just an effort to get people to spend money in South Carolina. But what's wrong with that? If you're going to spend money there anyway, it's kind of nice to start off with a good impression of the place.

Myrtle Beach, on what the promoters like to call "South Carolina's Grand Strand," is a fifty-mile-long strip of plastic next to a beautiful stretch of the Atlantic Ocean. The fast-food joints and chain motels are outshined only by the miniature golf courses, which tend toward large renditions of elephants, dinosaurs, and vehicles for space travel. There are, I am fairly sure, more pancake houses per capita in Myrtle Beach than anyplace else on the East coast. The place is a monument to plastic enfranchisement. Yet I like it, or at least short doses of it.

Maybe it helped that the season hadn't really started. It was chilly, and nobody was on the streets. There was a bright sun, and a clear blue sky, and the buildings looked freshly painted in anticipation of the coming summer. Many of them were painted white, and they reflected the brilliant light back and forth. I decided, as I walked around the main street and then headed toward the beach, that the reason I liked the place was that there were not yet too many people here. Somehow plastic is less awful—it even becomes almost interesting—when it isn't crowded like a K-Mart on a Saturday afternoon.

By the middle of the afternoon the temperature had risen five degrees, to perhaps the low seventies, and people started appearing on the streets. Particularly teenaged people. Where they had come from, I did not know. It was as if the slight increase in warmth had drawn them, involuntarily, out of their resting places. A juke box, which had been silent all morning, started to play "Hotel California." Two fads were enjoying great popularity at about that time; one was the Eagles' song, "Hotel California," and the other was the visage of a television creation with funny-looking hair, strangely-white teeth, and an erect right nipple. She bore the name Farrah Fawcett-Majors. While the juke box played "Hotel California" that afternoon in Myrtle Beach, Fawcett-Majors' face flashed from hundreds of posters and tee-shirts in the windows of trinket-and-suntan-oil stores.

The young people gathered in the open-fronted food-and-beer joints along the street that ran behind the beach, and they played the pinball machines and listened to the music. The most popular of the places was painted in bright reds and yellows, had a few dozen teenagers sitting at its picnic tables that were set back from the sidewalk, and seemed to be named "Chicken Boxes–Shrimp–Bar-B-Que-Chicken Box–Pepsi-Cola–Bar-B-Q–Breakfast 24 Hours a Day–Beer–Breakfast." It was selling, that afternoon, mostly soft drinks and hot dogs and beer. Across the street, in a place called "The Arcade," a siren that was connected to some electronic game went off from time to time, announcing a winner and attracting more losers.

The juke box in the place with the picnic tables was an advanced-model Seeburg that was so full of tacky colored plastic that it looked like the altar at some Southern California pet cemetery. Beside it stood the quintessence of the

Southern coastal teenager. She sang, along with the juke box, every syllable of "Hotel California."

She was the womanchild, a form of life that exists in every society, every region of the world, but that I remember from the South, and especially remember from my own youth there. I would not know her age—somewhere in her late teens, I suspect—but the actual number of years was unimportant. It was the stage of her life that mattered. Straight black hair that had been washed lately. A nose that was turned up a little at the end, the kind that people describe as "pert." A body that was young and far from ruined. Extremely faded bluejeans and bare feet.

The word that keeps coming back is *wantonness,* or perhaps *simulated wantonness.* The girl (and here we move, as did my thoughts that April afternoon as I sat at a picnic table in one corner and watched and listened, from that particular person to the millions of others who have gone through that same stage) wanted to look a little *wanton.* She was well-bred, from a good family that loved her. Did fairly well in school, but considered "wild" by her contemporaries and parents. She was the one who could blurt out fantastically outlandish things to the chemistry teacher and, most times, get away with it. Everything she does, every move she makes, is sensual, even when she has gone back to being a child for a moment and doesn't mean to be sensual at all. The girl ground her hips a bit to the music and sang along with it. She looked at the ceiling, and she knew that most everybody else was watching her.

A Typical American Family passed by on the sidewalk. Dad and Mom were in their late thirties. Junior was maybe thirteen. As they walked by the raucous teenage action, Dad looked only out of the corners of his eyes. He was a bit embarrassed; he knew he wasn't supposed to look at things like this. It was like going to a pornographic peep show; somebody you know might see you on the way out. Mom stared for a moment, the way women sometimes do when they're checking out the competition. The wild-looking teenage girl continued singing and grinding her hips, and she knew what was going on with the Typical American Family, probably because she came from one.

Junior was fascinated. He looked straight at the scene, without hangups, without embarrassment, pure interest and curiosity burning in his eyes. He lingered, almost stopped. His eyes had found the teenage girl now, and he was staring directly at her. Mom and Dad were hurrying along now; they wanted to be away from here. Mom's arm went back and her hand opened in a command. Junior took it and allowed himself to be pulled away. Already he was thinking about how, when he is on his own later in the day, or maybe tomorrow, he will come back here and look, and maybe learn, some more.

In the afternoons, at about 2:30, there are black ladies standing all along Ocean Boulevard. They are the cleaning ladies from the motels, and they are waiting for the bus to take them home from work.

"Home cooking," of course, is a part of the South. Sometimes it is delicious, sometimes it is fairly poisonous, but it nevertheless is decidedly authentic. I wanted some authentic food that night. Not knowing anything about the food situation in Myrtle Beach, I consulted a travel guide. It gave three stars, meaning "excellent," to a place that had a Southern-type name and that was referred to as "Popular." What really caught my eye, however, was the notation that the place had its "Own bread." Maybe a place that had Own bread was interested enough in food to have other authentic items in its kitchen.

I studied the menu. Sure enough, the bread was advertised as "home-baked." A waitress poured some wine for the couple at the next table and asked for their verdict. "Super," said the man. "It hits the spot," said the woman. Bad omens. Somehow I had never thought of wine's hitting the spot, or even being Super.

The bread came on a little wooden plank with its own serrated knife, and I knew I had been plasticized again. The little planks and knives were dead giveaways for a mass-produced product that is in wide restaurant use throughout the country: the non-home-baked individual loaf of "home-baked" bread. This particular version was called the Bridgford Demi-Loaf. At some point during the meal, which was quite short of impressive, the waitress asked me how it was. I suppressed the temptation to say "Super" or "It hits the spot" and mentioned that the bread was not "home-baked" and shouldn't really be advertised as such.

As I was paying the check, the owner of the place came over. He was distressed that I had not liked the bread. It *was* home-baked, he said, "because a little lady comes in every morning and bakes it." I said he was playing with words. The dough comes in frozen and pre-formed. And didn't it come from some factory hundreds of miles away? "It's from Pennsylvania, I think," volunteered the waitress. The owner said he thought it was from someplace else. I suggested that we find out. So the owner and I went to the huge walk-in freezer and looked at the piles of boxes of frozen "home-baked" bread. Each box contained twenty-seven and one-half pounds of pre-formed dough for the little lady to bake. It was manufactured in Anaheim, California, a place known to millions as the home of Mickey Mouse and Donald Duck.

The owner of the restaurant was very sporting about all this. He explained the economics of the restaurant business, which do not encourage low blood pressure, and then he threw out a very strong argument: Many, many people actually like that "home-baked" bread, regardless of the fact that it is three thousand miles from home. The owner had seen customers eat a few slices of the stuff, tuck the remainder into a purse or briefcase, and ask their waitress for more. Others, less larcenous, ask for doggie-bags—not for their steak, but for their leftover bread.

It was a pathetic comment on the eating habits of Americans, but I believed him. I'm certain that if we deprive people of real bread long enough, they'll soon start to enjoy the plastic variety.

A couple of mornings later I was leaving Myrtle Beach, and I visited the Diplomat Pancake House, in the motel of the same name, in search of a Thermos of coffee. While I waited I glanced at the menu. There was something about a "Hot Homemade Country Sausage Biscuit" for seventy-five cents.

I asked the gentleman at the cash register, who turned out to be Billy R. Smith, and the owner of the motel and restaurant, if the biscuits were "real." I was still smarting from the Demi-Loaf Affair.

"I'll show you how real they are," he said, and disappeared into the kitchen. He returned with his mother, Mrs. Eva Smith Caulder, who was seventy-eight years old, and who gets up early every morning to make the biscuits. Authentic biscuits, unfrozen biscuits, biscuits not from Anaheim.

Billy Smith had installed an ordinary, home-sized stove in his kitchen, alongside the giant professional ovens that turn out the pancakes and hash-browns, so his mother could bake her biscuits in the proper quantities. "If you mass-produce them," she said, "they *taste* like they're mass-produced." These were definitely not mass-produced. They were delicious. "Take you some preserves for your biscuits," said Mrs. Caulder. "They're home-made, too."

There was no great secret about how the biscuits were made. "I use Crisco all the time, and Red Band flour," said Mrs. Caulder. "And buttermilk. And I can use plain or self-rising flour, either one. But I can't give you my recipe because I don't measure anything. I sort of know how much to put in."

Mrs. Caulder has been baking biscuits for the general public in Myrtle Beach since 1939, when she moved her family to the coast from Charlotte. In those years she had operated a number of lodging places along the strand. The pancake house didn't even have a listing in the travel guide I carried, much less three stars. But it sure had "Own bread" and was "Popular." People came in and ordered bagsful of biscuits to go.

"Would you agree they're real enough?" asked Billy Smith. I was on my third biscuit and thinking about staying in Myrtle Beach another day so I could eat more. I replied that they were, and that the only thing that bothered me was whether this sort of food was on its way out, to be replaced by plastic dough from Disneyland.

"You're seventy-eight," I said to Mrs. Caulder, trying to be tactful but not exactly succeeding. "Presumably you're not going to be baking biscuits all that much longer. You'll be—retiring. What'll happen to those authentic biscuits then?"

"Call Rock, Billy," she said.

Billy Smith went to fetch Rock Smith, his twenty-eight-year-old son. Rock was a bright-looking young man with blue eyes and blond hair that he carefully maintains. He was a teenager when the hippies were in flower, and no doubt there were some people who thought he and his whole generation were beyond redemption. Now he had his hands in Crisco and Red Band flour every morning,

65

learning how to make proper, authentic biscuits like his grandmother.

I asked him why, and he replied that he liked the idea of carrying on a tradition. "And I enjoy giving people something good and satisfying to eat," he said. "If something like these biscuits are good, there ought to be somebody around to keep making them."

6

Out of the mainstream

A prime characteristic of the South is its propensity for legends. Austin country-rock singer, Atlanta urban success story, Tennessee sheriff frequently involved in violence—the region loves to create, believe in, and perpetuate myths, all of them planted, as myths should be, in a rich, but often quite shallow, topsoil of fact.

The most frequently quoted legends have been about the South itself, and of those, two have predominated. Cash, in *The Mind of the South,* identified them in 1941 as the legends of the Old South and of the New South. Both scenarios are familiar to anyone who has watched movies or listened to Chamber of Commerce orations. The Old South, said Cash, was thought to be populated by "gesturing gentlemen" who executed those gestures in "large and stately mansions" where the air was thick with "honor and chivalry and noblesse." (Somewhere to the rear of the mansions, of course, lived the blacks and the white trash.) The New South, when it appeared on the scene, was a thriving, modernized, industrialized society devoid of any trace of the Old South, "save for a few quaint survivals and gentle sentimentalities and a few shocking and inexplicable brutalities such as lynching. . . ."

Both legends contained some truth, of course, but neither was correct on its own. Cash's own view—and I think it holds equally true now, almost four decades later—was that the newer, more industrialized South "is a tree with many age rings, with its limbs and trunk bent and twisted by all the winds of the years, but with its tap root in the Old South."

Certainly one of the major characteristics of the Old South that has remained with the New is the quality we like to refer to as individualism. Southerners always have been, and continue now to be, more individualistically-inclined than most other Americans, with the possible exception of those from the non-urban Southwest. We resist authority—perhaps not so much because we detest it as because we refuse to take it seriously. We resist regimentation—unless it's in a military organization that promises the excitements of the hunt and the fight.

Traditionally the most individualistic of all Old Southerners, or at least the white ones, were those whom Cash called the "yeoman farmers"—hard-working, low-income people who didn't come from slave-holding families. Sometimes the yeomen were so individualistic that they left themselves wide open to exploitation by the planters, the banks, the railroads, and the textile mills (when they appeared on the landscape later in the nineteenth century). Many of the yeoman, and later their daughters and sons, went to work in the mills and were seriously exploited, in their pocketbooks and in their lungs, but rarely did they consider forming unions to improve their common situation. Unionism, by the twenties, was equated in many minds with communism and with that vast, despised category of suspicious stranger, often with dark curly hair and unfamiliar religious background, who was known as the "alien." And there was the fear among the lower-ranking whites that unionism would bring racial equality to the factory.

Unionism was, and still is, equated in the minds of many Southerners with something else, another concept that is more difficult to pin down, but that is nevertheless of immense importance—even when set alongside the low wages, pitiful fringe benefits, no job security, and contemptible health and safety conditions that characterize some Southern industries: it brought to quite a few workers the fear that somehow the *pride* would be taken out of their work; that a craftsperson would be reduced to a cog on a wheel; and that the end result would be a loss of individuality.

Politicians, industrialists, bankers, Chambers of Commerce, and others in the business of exploiting working people have been quick to light on these feelings in the South and to advertise them to prospective industries from elsewhere—industries that are considering a move, and that perhaps are tired of participating in struggles with organized labor. The exploiters speak universally of a "good labor climate," which, when translated, means an absence of union activity. In the eleven-state original Confederacy, only about fourteen percent of the workers are members of unions, while nationally the figure is around twenty-six percent. North Carolina and South Carolina have the lowest percentages in the region.

Of the twenty states in the nation with "right-to-work" laws, eleven, or the entire old Confederacy, are in the South. An example of how all this works may be found in an elaborate spiral-bound brochure published a few years ago by the Corpus Christi, Texas, Chamber of Commerce, and aimed at prospective industry. It speaks, more than anything else, of "a wealth of experienced labor eager to provide a good day's work for a good wage." So far, so good. That's a proper description of many, if not most, Southerners. But the brochure continues:

"The fair and equitable labor laws of Texas combine with the attitudes of South Texas workers to yield a stable labor environment. The incidence of crippling strikes and other unrest are minimized in Corpus Christi. The result is an enviable record in the past and the promise for a future that allows for getting the job done."

And what are those "fair and equitable labor laws of Texas"? Well, they're the ones that outlaw the agency shop and the union shop, restrict checkoff of dues, regulate picketing, outlaw a government agency from entering into a union contract, outlaw public employees from striking, forbid picketing to compel recognition or bargaining if the employees represent less than a majority, and others.

Texas always does things on a grander-than-necesssary scale, especially in areas where big business is concerned. But similar laws, and similar attitudes, prevail across the rest of the South—and many of those attitudes are based not only on what the bankers and mill-owners want done, but also on a distrust of organized labor by ordinary workers. They know that the labor movement is not a semi-religious force; they know that the Teamsters' Union is corrupt and has ties to the Mafia; they know that many union members "up North" seem to have lost all pride in their work and in themselves. The North serves as a source of much confirmation of the Southerner's fears about unionization. In New York City today, there is persuasive evidence that many of the workers most intimately involved with what is called, in political speeches and newspaper editorials, "the public trust"—the police officers, the schoolteachers, the hospital workers, the judges, the gravediggers—think of themselves more as members of unions than as professionals serving humanity, or even the portion of it that pays their salaries.

Southerners—not all of us, by any means, but enough, I think, to warrant the utterance of a broad, far-ranging statement—still have vastly different attitudes about work. They still care deeply about the *craft* of what they are doing, and they cling to this caring even as technology and modern business attitudes attempt to reduce the importance and quality of craftsmanship. A lot of my Northern friends, if asked what they think of the Southern worker, would reply that he or she is shiftless, a person whose work reflects his whole general demeanor, which (according to all the stereotypes, which my Northern friends, who get their information about the South from novels and movies, still believe) is one of unsophistication and subnormal educational accomplishment, mixed with hedonism. I know a Northerner who almost certainly thinks this way about Southerners, even though she herself comes to work at eleven in the morning, goes to lunch at noon, returns at three or three-thirty, and works incoherently (because of the liquid nature of the lunch) until four-thirty or so, when it's time to go home. And she holds a responsible job.

You simply cannot truthfully characterize Southerners as shiftless and lazy. Some, of course, are, but most are not. They may not talk all the time about how hard their work is, and they may not take pleasure in pinning ulcers and heart attacks on their chests as badges of their devotion to the grindstone, but they share a feeling about the essential decency of work that I do not see elsewhere in such abundance.

More than once I have heard Northern friends, just re-

turned from an automobile trip to the South, exclaiming
about the unexpectedly fine treatment they received at
the hands of some journey-person in Georgia or South
Carolina. In one case it was an ancient and deeply-loved
Mercedes-Benz, cream-colored and with a convertible top,
that came to a halt in Savannah. My friends briefly considered suicide, knowing that nobody within a thousand
miles could possibly fix the thing. A mechanic took the car
in, worked lovingly on it, fussed about my friends' accommodations while they waited, completed the repair, and
presented them with a bill so low they thought a mistake
had been made. The mechanic (and there are lots more
where he came from) obviously was guided by two principles: one, he was interested in the car—saw it as worth
fixing, saw it as a challenge to his craftsmanship, his ability to fix things; and two, he apparently thought not a
moment about my friends' vulnerability as being an opportunity to enrich himself.

It was a matter of *honor* with him, and how often can
you say that about automobile mechanics? Seldom, of
course. It's becoming even more seldom in the South now,
as elsewhere. But I think the tradition has lingered longer
in the Southland. People who *work* in the South have not
yet been reduced to numbers and cogs and ciphers and
bits of computer information and bored components of an
assembly line. Their psyches, their self-respect, haven't yet
been bruised beyond repair, as they have so definitely
been in the industrial North. These workers are helping
the South hold on a little longer to something that has
been all but discarded in the North.

Lots of Southerners who are concerned both about preserving the region's good qualities and promoting the economic progress of its citizens have been aware of all this
for a long time. Two of the many who are trying to do
something about it are Bill Finger and Bob Hall.

Bill Finger is a slow-talking man from Jackson, Mississippi, who, at the time I talked with him, was thirty years old and the staff director of Southerners for Economic Justice. The organization is based in Raleigh and has been supporting the effort to unionize the South's textile industry. Bob Hall, thirty-two and from Florida, puts out *Southern Exposure,* a well-edited and informative quarterly published by the Institute for Southern Studies, which has offices in Atlanta and Chapel Hill.

The Institute, whose founders include several whites who had been active in the civil rights and liberties movements of the Sixties, was started in 1970 "to analyze the region's social, economic, and political problems and to formulate alternative uses for its material and human resources." It, too, is deeply concerned about the textile industry. In the South that means being concerned about J. P. Stevens & Company, Incorporated, the most visible outlaw on the Southern labor scene today.

Stevens, the nation's second largest textile firm, is a multinational corporation that employs 44,400 people in eighty-five plants; eighty of them are in the South—and sixty-three in North and South Carolina. Not one Stevens employee was, by 1978, covered by a union contract and J. P. Stevens had demonstrated that it would do virtually anything to keep it that way. The United States Court of Appeals in New York has found the firm in contempt of court for what it called "massive violations" of the rights of its employees. Stevens, said the court, had the reputation of being "the most notorious recidivist in the field of labor law." Courts and labor tribunals have repeatedly found Stevens guilty of refusing to bargain in good faith and of intimidating employees who question its authority. It has been required to pay its illegally fired workers $1.3 million in back pay, and it has been found guilty of industrial piracy. It has settled out of court claims involving the under-reporting of taxes, price-fixing, and electronic eavesdropping on union organizers. It has repeatedly been accused of discriminating against workers on the basis of their race or sex, and of a massive lack of concern for the safety of the employees it *does* hire. J. P. Stevens's headquarters is on Sixth Avenue in New York City. The firm shows no signs of wanting to change its ways and stop acting like a Central American dictatorship. It is a fine example of what people are up against when they talk about improving the lot of the Southern worker.

Bob Hall, like many of us who are from the South, is a Southern chauvinist. "It's great to be alive in the South today," he said when I saw him and Bill Finger in Chapel Hill. Then, like so many of us, he moved swiftly from his exultation to his fears about the future of his homeland. Southerners do this a lot, you know; we still care about our region.

"Life in the South used to be arranged around personal relationships and kinship patterns," said Hall. "That arrangement cut through everything: through racial relationships, economic relationships, political relationships, religion, everything. But we're now in the process of a transition to a point where life is only organized around money. What's becoming more and more important in the South is how you relate to dollars and cents: if you've got it or, if you don't have it, how you can get it. Because money is now the thing that makes a difference for people. It's been defined that way: success or failure, good and bad. All the values, in my mind, are becoming twisted and corrupted by the decadence of being able to get some money in your hands. This is one of the last places where it is happening, but I see it happening.

"It's a kind of an atomization of the South, where everybody's most important thing is to see how much money they can make and how they can get ahead. The easy style of living disappears; the competitive framework of life is entering in."

The offspring of Cash's yeoman farmer, said Hall, now

find themselves strangely in the middle of all this. Some are following their elders into the textile mills. Among blacks, quite a few are entering the mills. But many of the young people, who in earlier times might have stayed on the farm, are absorbed now into the service-industry jobs in the cities and pseudo-suburban cities of the South. They're pumping gas, and working in motels and restaurants and shopping centers, and selling insurance on commission.

It is into this situation, said Bill Finger, that textile union organizers have moved—trying to convince workers that a decent wage, a modicum of job security, and a little dignity are not going to rob them of their individualism. It is a difficult undertaking. The organizers, if they are to be as sensitive as Finger and others would wish, must deal not only with the traditional economic issues and the illegal actions of firms such as J. P. Stevens, but also with the "positive Southern values"—the ones that make Southerners different from other people. In a way, orthodox unions are not prepared for such a task.

"You see," said Hall, "the union is involved in this in a very complicated way. It's not a force for maintaining community harmony in the traditional sense. It is also (along with business and government) involved in a rationalization of the economy and the work situation. The union is looking for getting better conditions, better dollars and cents for people. They're not as concerned about, and their tradition is not as involved in, the Southern way of looking at what work means. They view work in terms of a Northern, or capitalistic, attitude."

The unions are, then, in a sense, outsiders?

"Yes," replied Finger. "In a nutshell, a lot of their decisions are made in New York and a lot of the people who're affected are in the South."

One tremendous first step in improving the lot of the Southern worker, said Finger, would be to guarantee him a decent system for arbitrating his job grievances. There are relatively few such systems in the South now, and Finger feels their presence would go a long way toward providing the Southern worker with the dignity—the individualism—he or she deserves. He said: "The key place, I think, where some of the union officials can nurture some of the positive Southern values, or at least allow them to develop in this kind of institutional protection system, is in the arbitration system. Because then people *do* have a way to get recourse. They don't have to take any shit any more."

I asked what the system was now.

"There is none. Anything you do, you can get fired. And there's no protection. None.

"The union is sensitive to the fact that they're viewed as outsiders," Finger said, speaking mainly of the textile workers' union. "And the questions that the people ask of the organizers are fresh and new, and they're trying to organize in a way that is responsive to Southern workers. The whole thing of personal dignity is a major thing when you're trying to organize Southern workers. What Southern workers want is a sense of persona, of dignity, when they work. It used to be that the company had a facade of personal relationships and paternalism. In the winter the mill owner'd give them a winter coat. But they don't do that any more. They treat them like a part of a machine. And that attitude is what is pushing the Southern worker to find recourse in a union."

We talked a good deal longer, and I became more and more impressed by the obvious *belief* that Bob Hall and Bill Finger had in the South. In other parts of the country, people and organizations were concerned about somewhat more narrowly defined causes—about the labor movement, or health care, or quality education, or job opportunities for minorities, or abstract painting, or disco dancing. Here were two men—representative of thousands more—who were concerned about *the South,* and about the qualities that made it good and that they wanted to preserve. They were painting a somewhat painful picture of a region where individualism was under severe attack. Did they feel it would be eventually wiped out?

"I don't think so," said Hall. "So many of the objective conditions are still there, at least in the case of the smaller Southern cities. The institutions are not all going to change overnight. It's like asking if blacks are going to become totally amalgamated into the American mainstream as a race, or as a sub-culture. I don't think it's ever going to happen, to blacks or to the South.

"But for the *most part* it's going to happen. The trick is to try to preserve enough of those traditions and enough leaders who have roots in those traditions so that, at a time when they become important again, and when more people become alienated from that money-centered new style of life, that their imaginations are still there."

And the traditions and qualities that should be preserved?

"Things like rage, and personal anger, and imagination," said Hall. "Those are some of them. The imagination that created the kind of writers who come from the South. And the sense of language, and the sense of feel for things. Those are important things that industrialization, mechanization, and automation can beat out of people—systematically root it out of people. You can become mesmerized and lose all sense of passion. And passion in the South is something that should be continued."

"More and more people," said Finger, "are being drawn into government jobs and becoming dependent on them. This sucks people into the government arena, and that homogenization, then, seeps down to more and more people. And they don't have to use their imagination as much. I could see this happening to myself. If I got enough passion beat out of me, I could see where I would go to government to get a job. And then I know I'd be okay, financially."

Bob Hall agreed. "A lot of it is actually beaten out of people. You become droned down so that television is the ultimate relaxation. Nothing is required of you any more. Any other form of relaxation requires energy, and it's energy and willpower that are being pulled out of you."

I assume, I said, that even though you're pessimistic you believe the South is the best place in the country?

"Oh, yes, I do," said Finger.

"It's *our* place," said Hall. "It's not 'better' or 'worse.' It's the place we have. We are in it. The South is not in the mainstream. Being where we are, we can look at the mainstream a little more objectively. Hopefully, some of the assets of the South will improve the mainstream.

"But we're not trying to say that the South is a great place and everything in it is pure. Racism is very strong, still. And just at the point where people were beginning to deal with it, when they have to deal with a whole 'nother load of crap—all these new factories moving in and all these new politicians. There's nothing pure about the South, but the possibilities that the South offers for us are a lot better than the possibilities in a lot of other places. Because the possibilities in the other places have been eliminated, rooted out."

"There's still a chance," said Finger, "for the people who call the shots—in the financial, industrial, labor and cultural worlds—to be sensitized to some of the same issues we're talking about. And I think some of them are, and they can talk about the same things we're talking about—the rage, and anger, and passions being beaten down. These are the people who *control* the way money is invested and jobs are developed. I think the South still has enough open space, still has cities that are manageable and small enough to be comfortable places to live in."

There's still time in the South, he was saying. I've heard the expression so often in these journeys. *There's still time to do it right. To make the South what it should be. To save the South.*

"And that's why we're working with the textile union," said Bob Hall. "Because unionization's the next big thing that's going to happen in the South in the next ten years. And we want to try to make it happen better than it happened in the North.

"Not only that: but to happen in a way that would *ignore* how it has gone on elsewhere. To begin afresh and say, 'Okay, if we're going to work all these hours, how do we want our work to be arranged?' And just start all over again and do it right."

7

Full spring

James A. Graham is an old-fashioned commissioner of agriculture, or at least that is the image he likes to convey. He wears a pearl-grey Stetson, sounds gruff, and can speak for quite some time without yielding to an interruption. He is a politician. Last time he ran for re-election, he carried ninety-seven out of North Carolina's one hundred counties, and he got a greater percentage of the vote than anyone else who was running.

On his desk is an ashtray shaped like a tobacco leaf, a symbol of North Carolina's heavy investment in the growing, manufacturing, promoting, and selling of cancer sticks. (You might like to know that Americans, in 1976, sucked the smoke of 620,000,000,000 of them deep into their lungs.) There is also a large gold peanut, and on the wall a portrait of two mules. The mule motif is carried out elsewhere in the commissioner's office, but the visitor's eye is more quickly drawn to Graham's desk pen set, which has a gold hog standing in its middle. The production of pork is becoming increasingly important in North Carolina's agricultural economy.

Graham is, perhaps as much as anything else, a figure of transition in agriculture. He is old-fashioned, running a state government department that still carries out many of the tasks it performed decades ago, when my father was its self-taught auditor. Graham is old-fashioned in other ways as well; during a conversation he managed to refer to "Three of my marketing people, one little lady and two people . . . ," and he seemed to be genuinely confused when I asked if women weren't people too.

But he also runs an agency that is heavily into agribusiness, and that means new-fashioned. There existed in the old South a phenomenon known as the "two-mule farmer." He and his family had enough land on which to get by, and they could farm it with two mules. None got rich that I know of, except those whose farms lay in the paths of interstate exits and who sold out to Howard Johnson and Big Mac, and those who supplemented their agricultural income with a crop of stills back in the woods. But there is a great deal of mourning in the South for the passing of the two-mule farmer, and I suspect much of it is based on a distrust of agribusiness. One difference between agribusiness and agriculture, after all, is the difference between business and culture.

"Only about five per cent of the people are really farming in this state now," Graham was saying. He can recite statistics and percentages like a New York Yankees fanatic. "We used to have more farmers than any other state in the nation except Texas. But now we're fourth."

And the farmers who were left, I asked; what about them?

"You've got a different man out there," he said. "It used to be a small farmer with a mule, a cow, a plow, a sow, and fifty chickens."

And now?

"What is it now? You've got a man out there who could have *five hundred* cows or *five hundred* sows. But he won't have a *single* cow or sow. Everything has changed a great deal—the methods of working, the money invested."

How much money *is* invested now?

"Well, a man was in here yesterday, wanting me to help him get some financing. He was talking about a hundred ninety-five thousand dollars to go into the turkey business. They say in a dairy operation today, you're talking about a quarter-of-a-million to get started."

And what did it cost in the past?

"Back then, a good mule cost you two-fifty, three hundred dollars. And a plow cost you sixty-five or seventy. Maybe three or four thousand dollars to get into business.

"We used to think in terms of counties," said the commissioner. "Counties and regions, like the West, the mountains, the Piedmont, the Southeast, the Northeast. Now we think about North Carolina as a whole state. And we're talking about not only states, and the *United* States, but we're talking about the whole world. Because agriculture and agribusiness is the most important factor today, because of reciprocal trade, and oil, and everything. We're looking towards international markets instead of domestic markets.

"Agriculture is not just one area any more. It's a fantastic, fan-tas-tic, FAN-TAS-TIC thing with a tremendous future."

I guess I was more interested in the past and the present than the future. I asked him how the shift from small farms to agribusiness had affected things.

"It's had an effect on everything," he said. "The school

system, transportation, everything. And in some cases, I think, the effects are not good. We're losing that desire— what is the word I want? That *independence*. It's had an effect on our amenities, our development, our churches and religious life, our educational life. In some areas it's good and in some areas it's not. I hate to see some of these smaller communities disappear.

"I'll tell you something that really bothers me. That's a ghetto. You know what the new ghetto of the South is going to be? The mobile home. The South is full of them. The reason is credit. A young couple goes out today, all they can buy is a mobile home. They can't afford a house. You can buy a mobile home like you can buy a car.

"And I'm concerned about the changes. We're still basically an agrarian state, but we're rapidly vanishing from that. And I'm concerned about what we're going to go through before we learn to maintain a balance. I don't think we've found it yet. I think we're getting away from the balance."

Graham talked on about computers—he disliked them, but his agriculture department used them—and stupid rules imposed by Washington bureaucrats on decent working people, and I asked him if he wasn't part of a dying breed. He said yes, he was.

"These ideas are going," he said. "They're slowly dying a death like a frog in warm water. You throw a frog in *hot* water and he'll jump out of there. He won't stay there very long. But you put him in *warm* water, and soften him up a little bit, and he'll just sit there while you slowly cook him.

"I wonder what your father would say if he could come back and see all the computers and agribusiness stuff now. Poor thing, I think it'd give him a heart attack. He wouldn't last long in this situation now. He'd get pretty damn mad at that computer."

He was surely right about my father, and he was right about the mobile homes. All through the countryside where the two-mule farms once had been, people now lived in mobile homes. It is easy to talk about how ugly the devices are, and easy to forget that such homes are really all a lot of people can afford. But the ugliness! Other generations have constructed housing that was thought of, in its day, as ordinary or perhaps even tacky, only to be rediscovered forty, sixty, a hundred years later as beautiful, utilitarian works of art. I have tried to project my thoughts into the future and fantasize that the classic American mobile home, its shape hardly more pleasing to the eye than the back end of a moving van, will someday be appreciated. So far, I have been unsuccessful. The mobile home will always be ugly. Perhaps the ugliest one of all time is the one I saw in eastern North Carolina. One end had brown plastic strips mounted on it, to give it a pseudo-Tudor look. The adjacent side had pink plastic tiles mounted on it to make it look pseudo-Spanish.

The houses are awful enough by themselves, but they are even worse when they stand, as they often do, next to an old frame country house out along the farm roads. The old house sits there comfortably, two stories tall with high ceilings and chimneys at both ends, a large porch out front for rocking and swinging and watching, a tall oak or pecan tree in front. Beside it, the flat, harshly-angled mobile home, its ceiling low, its intestines arranged shotgun-style, infernally hot in the summertime and incredibly cold in the winter, resting on cinder blocks, the tank of propane or kerosene outside, a pickup with CB antenna parked in the front yard. The old house may still be in partial use; more than likely its windows are all gone. The people who live in the mobile home are the grandsons and granddaughters of the people who built the old house;

they lived in the house, as much for old times' sake as any-thing else, until their parents died. Then they bought the mobile home.

The farm around their odd-looking little compound may be all daisies and milkweed. The residents don't work the place, except for a small vegetable garden. They work—husband and wife—in the nearest town, or on the highway leading into it. They work at the Sears store, or the car-repair place, or the mill.

And these are the old houses that are still standing. Countless others are abandoned, empty; falling or fallen down. Many are just brick chimneys, rising out of foun-dations that were built to last forever.

A less sad picture: a blue-collar suburb of a medium-sized Southern city, out on land that once was pasture. A road runs through it, busy from taking the people back and forth to the shopping center and the school. Off the road runs a driveway, and in the driveway there is a mail-box mounted on an old plow. It is the kind of plow that mules used to pull. There are snapdragons and morning-glories growing around the plow. At the other end of the driveway is a mobile home. The owner has painted the structure deep red, obviously in an effort to make it blend in more with its surroundings. And the plow? Was it a souvenir of an earlier existence? Of pleasant memories, or unpleasant ones?

An alternative to the mobile homes in their country and suburban settings would be the downtown of a sizeable city—say Charlotte. I was there on an earlier trip, one in which I was relying on the airlines for transportation, and I liked the looks of the place. Not too big, not too crowded, decent housing available within the city limits, plenty of opportunities for recreation nearby, awful-tasting water but you probably got used to it.

Late in the afternoon I finished my meetings, in an office building near the center of town, and headed for my hotel. The people I was with talked about giving me a ride or calling a taxi, but the Sheraton was visible out the office window, certainly no more than a mile away. I grabbed my small suitcase and started walking.

The sidewalk ran out after a short while, because few people walk in Charlotte any more. Everyone was in automobiles and was heading for the suburbs. Their faces were grim, their windows rolled up, and the sight of me, a pedestrian, walking in their gutter because there was no sidewalk, actually frightened some of them. What was a person doing *walking* on this street? Some of the drivers furtively drank beers in little paper sacks. Some drank beers without any attempt at disguising the fact. Some seemed blissed out; they were listening, no doubt, to their eight-tracks, turned up very high to drive away the pain of a day spent being a cog in someone else's machine. They were heading home. By the time I got to the Sheraton, downtown Charlotte was practically deserted, except for the black people and the whites who didn't have cars and who had to wait for the public transportation. Except for a few essential services—the getting out of a newspaper, the operation of a movie house or two, the sale of some sandwiches in a Greek luncheonette, Charlotte was closed.

I got to the hotel, which sat on what was obviously some urban renewal land, put there like some stupid Howard Johnson's out on a toll road. I say obviously urban renewal land because it was too flat, too squared-off; the grass was too green, the trees too sparse. Obviously real human beings, albeit those at the lower ranges of the economic scale, had lived in this part of town until the urban renewal money had arrived from Washington. Then, if it happened here as it had happened everywhere else in the country, the despised people were chased out, banished forever. The land became dusty parking lots at first, and then someone announced great plans for a shopping center or something. The plans fell through; some of the land went to the congloms like the Sheraton, while the rest just sits there, looking phony. And no one knows what became of the people who used to live there.

The hotel had never heard of my reservation. But it eventually got straightened out. Even more eventually I got the key to my room, took the elevator up, unlocked the door, and discovered another tenant in the bathroom. He was taking a shower. Back to the front desk, where they gave me the key to another room. The apology was sort of half-hearted, even less sincere than the one the airlines give when they lose your baggage, and I got the impression that my experience was not all that unique.

The situation perked up that night. I discovered an authentic Indian restaurant with authentic Indian food prepared and served by authentic Indian people. I also discovered a boor at the table next to me. He embarrassed his wife, the employees, and anyone else who could hear him by ragging the waiter about the items on the menu, pronouncing them foolishly, and in general displaying his ignorance. He felt out of his depth, I supposed, so he sought to shift the nervousness to his host. I suppose he felt it helped that his host had brownish skin. I prefer, though, to remember the meal, which was delicious. How it happened that such a place existed in Charlotte I'll never know, but I know that it could *only* have happened in a city.

On the way to the airport the next morning, dark-cold in that cruel half-hour or so before the sun comes up, I consulted the cab driver. The drivers of taxis are widely considered to be the founts of all wisdom. This, of course, is not true, as one can tell from talking fifteen seconds with a New York cabbie. But I asked the man, anyway, if he felt a part of the downtown business development. We had just passed through the center of the city and there were, in addition to the urban renewal scars, several striking office-building-and-hotel–works-in-progress of the sort that have become *de rigeur* for cities that wish to be certified as progressive.

"Well, I tell you," he said. "Charlotte used to be low and kind of grey-looking, something that you sort of couldn't be proud of. Now they're doing all this building. I *want* to feel like I'm a part of it. I really do. It's nice to be able to look at the tall buildings, and the new buildings, and to think that they're kind of *yours*, when you've lived in a place all your life like I have."

Moving again. On a later trip through Charlotte, this time by car, I discovered the ultimate in enfranchised plastic: at a fast-food joint that appears to be locally popular, they serve you a hot dog—a *hot dog*, mind you—in a little styrofoam coffin. Those plastic boxes have been used for some time, of course, for plasticburgers, but a *hot dog?* I wondered what percentage of the cost of the total package, as they say on Madison Avenue, went for styrofoam and what percentage went for hot dog?

Not two miles away, on the same highway, the transition started. It is one that I see from time to time in the South but rarely in the North: a fairly abrupt shift from a densely-packed urban area, with parking lots and used cars and places that would sell you hot dogs in styrofoam boxes, to the vestiges of a rural area. I say vestiges because that is all they are: mere traces of a culture that once existed in this geographical area, but that now has either been eliminated or pushed much farther out into the countryside. What it *really* is, in so many cases, is the refusal by one or maybe two landowners, who have watched the city and its suburbs grow and encroach through the years, to give up their little plots of country. And so, if the land is not, in the eyes of the city and suburbs, worth condemning, the eccentric landowners will be humored ("The old son of a bitch will be dead in a year or two, anyway, and the heirs'll be sure to sell out to us") and the development, the progress, the American dream, will continue on around and past them.

This particular four-lane was laced with Kentucky Fried Chicken and This Mall and That Mall, and muffler shops and broadloom joints, all so undistinguished that the commuters could drive past them morning and evening without even seeing them. But there was one patch of undeveloped grass, within viewing and walking distance (if there had been sidewalks) of the tallish buildings that were beginning to make downtown Charlotte distinguishable from the rest. And in the middle of that acre of grass, paying absolutely no attention to the commuters, was a horse, grazing.

Passing on a Saturday through a lovely college town, one of those with Tradition and Heritage and cannonballs all over the campus, I saw about a dozen students lined up in front of a bank. Lining up in front of a theater I could understand, and maybe even a beer hall if it were truly popular, but a bank? I looked closer and saw they were waiting their turn to punch their numbers into the sidewalk money machine, so they could get enough bread to take them through the weekend.

It was early the following afternoon, a Sunday, when I passed the county prison farm. It had strong-looking, but probably quite vulnerable, fences and guard towers that were not all occupied. I wouldn't have noticed it except for the lines of people waiting alongside the fence. Perhaps two dozen people, looking ordinary and middle-aged like many of the rest of us, were standing beside the highway, on the narrow shoulder between the fence and the pavement, waiting for visiting hours to start.

One of them was different. She was a nice-looking young woman—her youth was what made her different from the others—and she was wearing very tight, very faded blue jeans. She was not chatting with the others or looking across the highway, the way the other waiting people were doing. Rather she was holding onto the fence with both hands, grabbing it very tightly as if it were responsible for holding her up. And she was gazing in toward the ugly prison buildings as if she were trying to see through the walls.

It was full spring now. A front had moved through, and the air was clear and chilly and the sky was the clear, crisp blue of fall, but the color of the foliage gave it away. The leaves of the trees and bushes were green, a fresh green, a new green that obviously had just been born, a green that was going to last the whole summer.

And the man in the field gave it away. His tractor was parked by the shoulder of the highway, its harrow attached to it. He had finished plowing, and now he was planting. Patiently but firmly he strode the plowed lines, throwing seeds upon the ground. He carried the seeds in a burlap sack that he had altered so it would fit around his shoulders, like a sort of a sling. He walked rhythmically, like a ballet dancer, his progress across the field one unbroken fluid act of stepping, reaching into the bag, and casting his right arm through a graceful arc.

In the mountains, where I was heading, it was very

much spring. For two days there had been thunderstorms and tornadoes, and now the streams were in flood. It happens every spring in the mountainous parts of Virginia, North Carolina, West Virginia, Kentucky, and Tennessee. Houses are carried away by the waters (and people return, this time with mobile homes, and start living again on precisely the same spot. When the slick television reporters ask them why, they invariably reply, "Because we don't have anyplace else to go," or "Because this is my home."). The thunderstorms and tornadoes wipe people off the face of the earth without their ever knowing what happened. This had happened the day before to the people in an airliner outside Atlanta.

Spring is a violent time of the year. It is as if nature (here I go, anthropomorphizing again) doesn't want to give up on winter; as if nature knows how much we desire spring and warmth and decides to tease us for a few more weeks; as if spring is being born under great pain and with great violence, by Caesarian section.

The road rose steeply now, into the mountains, and as it did the water became abundant. It cascaded down the mountains, creating waterfalls where later in the summer the rocks would be dry; stopping for nothing on its way to the sea. Spring was running later here than at the coast; the dogwood here was just beginning to bloom, while down on the coastal plain it had already leafed out.

The mountains were purple-blue; the roads were serpentine and beautiful. I passed a turnoff for Church of God Road and kept climbing. All of a sudden, I realized I had ascended into a new zone of climate and geography. I was up along the crest of the Blue Ridge now, and I had left spring behind. All of a sudden I could see through the trees, because there were no leaves. I don't know where the

9 1

line of demarcation was; I had just gone around the side of a mountain and had slipped back into the tail end of winter.

Chilhowie calls itself the Apple Center of Southwest Virginia. It is close to an interstate (one of the few such highways that isn't ugliness personified) and on a more meandering road that precedes the interstate. Through the town runs a stream, which isn't even represented on the official state highway map, that was one of those that flooded. The water passed along swiftly among the roots and lower branches of hundreds of trees that once had stood well back from the banks, and when I drove through there was evidence that, not long before, the water had been much higher: dozens, hundreds of pieces of mud-stained plastic, of the consistency and transparency of dry-cleaning bags, were hanging from the upper branches of the trees. They clung there, web-like, as if they had been spun by spiders.

The sun declined to come up the next morning. Fog and drizzle covered the land, and spring once again was moved off into the future. I was filling the tank at a gas station when a young man, with the talk and gait of a mountain person, came in and told his friend at the station that some son of a bitch had stolen the carburetor out of his car during the night. There was talk about how low someone would have to stoop to do a nasty thing like that.

"What you going to do about it?" asked the man in the gas station.

"You can shore bet," said the young man, "that *I'm* going to go out tonight and get *me* a carburetor and get even."

8

West, over the mountains

I made it to New Market, Virginia, on the western side of the lovely Shenandoah Valley, not far from the West Virginia line. The places here had pleasant-sounding names, like Shenandoah and Front Royal and Woodstock. Farther south and west, as the elevation increased and the coal mines proliferated, the names took on harder edges, like Keokee, Stonega, Pardee, Clinchco, and Grundy.

New Market was trying to change its image and it had not completely succeeded. There was a sign that welcomed you to Historic New Market, and next to it was a fine-looking old house whose façade was largely given over to advertisements directing you to places other than New Market. Two minutes to the north, said one, would bring you to Spaghetti, Pizza, and Chicken in the Rough. Three miles in the same direction would reward you with Dr.

Childress's Snake and Monkey Farm. Another mile and you'd hit Shenandoah Caverns. I went in the other direction.

David Stolz, Nannie Zirkle, and Mary Alladdin sat on Mrs. Zirkle's front porch on the main street, not far from the center of town. The South is many things to many people; some of those things are good and some are bad, but one of the best things about it is its front porches. From the high galleries of Savannah and Charleston, where the rice-planters sat in the summertimes to watch the evening breezes and avoid the malaria, to the simple, functional additions to the cabins in the Appalachian hollows, porches have been places where much of Southern life is lived.

New Market was quiet that day. On the main street a policeman sat in a tilted-back chair on the sidewalk in front of the police station, the door of his patrol car open so he could hear the radio. This was his front porch, at least until he got home. And a few doors away, David and Nannie and Mary sat on their sunny porch and watched life go by. Not much went by. I stopped at the grocery down the street to get food to take across the mountains into the woods of West Virginia, and on my way back to the car I said hello to them.

Mary Alladdin wasn't at all shy about talking. She had had, she said, right off the bat, a hard time of it. "They threw me out and put me on the road," she said, and it was clear that she was speaking of some people to whom she had owed some money. She didn't say where this had happened, or when. The fact of its happening, though, very much occupied her mind now. "I was less than a hundred dollars behind on my payments," she said. "It was twenty-three sixty-nine a month on a thousand-dollar loan. They threw me out on the street." Now she was boarding at Mrs. Zirkle's house. She had a wonderfully kind face and long reddish-blonde hair and smiled all the time. Her eyes were lovely and alive.

"I sing and write country music," she said, "My philosophy is sort of standing up for your nation and the principles on which the nation was founded." David Stolz smiled, as if maybe he had heard Mary speak on this subject before, but it was a polite, respectful smile, as if he didn't especially mind hearing it again. Mrs. Zirkle said nothing, and I think it was because she was hard of hearing. A couple of cars passed by on the street, heading in the direction of the snakes, monkeys, chickens, and caverns. As they passed the police station the officer gave them the standard, professional once-over with his eyes.

"I'm sort of a freedom fighter," said Mary. "I believe in protesting like the devil to preserve the rights of all people. This is what General Lee was trying to do. I'm a community-action person, I guess you might say."

I asked her about her music, and she responded by singing the first song she had written. It was titled "Baby Boy." She said she had written it before the people at a television series that was then popular, "Mary Hartman, Mary Hartman," had written *their* song of the same name. Then she sang what she considered her best song, one about a letter from a soldier in Vietnam to his mother. Both her songs were very nice. They were songs that most of the people of the country could understand and appreciate. Representatives of the Literary Establishment wouldn't like them at all.

"I can sing all kinds of music," she said. She smiled constantly. "It's just a gift. You can overcome all your hardships, you know, if you want to. My first love is for God and in what God would have me do. I don't take dope, drink, or smoke, and I'm giving up coffee. All I need is a break. I want to get into the country music business, and all I need is a break, a contact." She looked me straight in the eye. "Maybe God sent you to give me that break."

I told Mary Alladdin that I suspected God employed a better Messenger service. Then I said: "It's interesting, what you said about overcoming your hardships—"

"That's right," she said, breaking in politely. She stood up. "I bet you didn't even notice my arm. I lost it in an accident in a launderette. Some people would have just sat down and cried and let life go by. But I've overcome it."

The long right sleeve of her blouse floated in the air like a dandelion puff. I *had* noticed it, some minutes earlier. That was why I started to ask the question about hardships. But that wasn't important. What was important was that Mary Alladdin had overcome it. She was smiling broadly as she sat there on that sunny front porch and waited for her big break.

They hardly ever get that break, I thought, as I headed west from New Market, up toward the mountains. Mary Alladdin was a member of a very large community of Southern Americans—actually, of *American* Americans, but you see more of them in the South—who might best be described as constituting the long-suffering America.

In the rush of this nation toward industrialization, mechanization, urbanization, and now suburbanization, certain people are left behind. Some remain of their own free will; some stay because they are uncomfortable, confused, unwanted in the new society that is being created. I am not saying that Mary Alladdin fit into any of those specific categories, for I did not get to know her well enough to tell, but I do know that she reminded me of the long-suffering America.

Back when I worked on *The Atlanta Journal*, we'd take

turns holding down the news desk on Saturday nights. The Sunday paper had long since been locked up and was rolling out of the place as fast as the trucks could carry it, but someone had to be around in case the world ended or Christ returned. The phone rang a lot, but with few flashes and bulletins. A lot of the people who called were folks who got drunk once a week, and, when they did, a lot of venom came out, so they'd call us and accuse us, in language that might be regarded as indelicate, of being pro-integration. (The reporters were, of course. The people who ran and owned the paper thought only about making money, as far as I could tell.)

But some who called were the long-sufferers. They were people whose pensions had been taken away; who had been told, after a lifetime of putting money into Social Security, that they weren't eligible; who had been ripped off by some insurance salesman or encyclopedia company. People who had been caught and mangled in the maw of modern society, just as surely as Mary Alladdin had been mangled. They were the victims. And I cannot help but remember that when I hung up the phone, after giving them the best advice I could, I'd occasionally make fun of them—crack some joke about them with the others who sat at the desk, pushing along the late sports scores and waiting for the end of the world or the Second Coming or one A.M., whichever came first. And later I'd feel guilty about blaming the victims, and sorry that I had not been able to help them.

The road got narrower and rougher as it went up toward the crest of the mountain that formed the boundary between Virginia and West Virginia. I stopped at a combination general store–gas station–post office and asked if I were headed the right way.

"Well, where is it exactly that you want to go?" the combination grocer–service station operator–postmistress asked me.

"To the little campground just over the West Virginia line." I produced a Forest Service map and pointed out the place.

"Oh," she said. "That's over the mountain." As if only a fool with a beard and New York license plates would want to go *over the mountain*.

Later I saw what she may have meant. The road went from paved to tar with gravel in it to regular tar to regular gravel, then to dirt, and all the time it was getting narrower and narrower. It was down to one lane when I met Alvie Siever and his relatives, the Ritchies. I stopped to ask them if I were on the right road. The map showed it as a solid black line, but it seemed to be getting pretty dotted to me. Alvie and the Ritchies all wore the faces of honest hill people.

I asked them, after a while, if they considered themselves Southerners. Alvie Siever removed, then replaced, his cap and folded his arms over his bib overalls. "I guess we are," he said after thinking about it a while. "But it'd be better to say we were *mountain* people."

The campground was primitive and stark-empty, which is the way I like them, except that in the middle of the night some cretin came in and fired up a portable generator, which is illegal, and then shut it down and disappeared after half an hour. Also in the middle of the night something went crashing around through the woods about fifty yards away, in the vicinity of the stream. In these mountains there is only one animal that you generally refer to as "crashing around."

I woke early the following morning and lay in the tent,

watching the sun head up on the other side of the notch that led to Virginia; and I saw how green West Virginia is. Huge portions of the state have been raped by industry— by Allied Chemical and its henchfirms, by companies that make dumb-looking "now" fabrics out of coal tar, by places that fill the rivers and skies with the worst sorts of filth. But other portions of West Virginia, like the one I happened to be staring at right now, seem to be as green and fresh and primitive as they must have been in their infancy.

In other places where I have erected my tent, I have had the feeling—a mixture of regret and relief—that I was in a place where many humans have been before. Regret because that means (incorrectly) that there is nothing more to discover; relief because I know that if others have been here and survived, then I can too. But in West Virginia it is still possible to have the feeling (quite likely an incorrect one, too) that you are standing someplace where no one else has stood.

I folded the tent, fixed breakfast, inspected the car for damage (the last mile or so had been on a rock trail and across a couple of creeks, without bridges), decided that slightly upcurved tailpipes looked *good* on a Beetle, and set off for Tennessee.

Knoxville lay beneath a foul sea of polluted yellow air, and I regretted having to spend the night there. The cleaning lady at the motel said it happened quite often. The clerk at the desk said it must be coming from the mountains and that it was some kind of a haze. Obviously it was human-made. It smelled the way plastic smells when you burn it. The air was so thick that the tall masts that support gasoline company signs on the interstate— support them high, so they'll be seen for great distances—

were not themselves visible. Huge Exxons and Gulfs seemed to hang there in the atmosphere, an atmosphere that was yellow-thick with the burned products of Exxon and Gulf. I headed west as fast as I could, adding my little bit to the pollution.

I took a break for lunch at a rest stop on Interstate 40, the road that runs the length of Tennessee. Quite a few other people had done the same thing. Two older couples sat at the picnic table near me, and one of the women, a pleasant-looking lady in an immaculate white pants suit, got up and inspected a device that came out of the ground. It looked like an old-fashioned water pump. She touched the handle and water squirted furiously from it.

Obviously it was a modern water faucet, disguised as an old-fashioned pump. "My goodness," said the woman. "It's a lot easier than the pump we grew up with on the farm."

The roadside signs that used to say "See Rock City" were almost nonexistent on the interstate. Instead there were the signs for Stuckey's, and Day's Inn, and Holiday Inn, and KOA. There were quite a few places that were essentially automotive and truck service stations with attached cafes. Do we really want to buy our meals from gas stations?

Nashville was all greenery and rolling hills and fast-moving traffic, constantly blending and merging like that of a city ten times its size. The air was still filthy. A place called The Grecian Inn asked that I try its spaghetti dinner, and another billboard announced that a famous country singer had opened a plastic-looking "country store." Barefoot nymphets in tight, faded cutoffs stood on a traffic island advertising a civic-club car wash. I stopped on an almost-deserted road and helped a very slow turtle cross the pavement.

It was Saturday night, and I went looking for the Nashville Sound. Nashville, of course, is the home of the Grand Ole Opry, and it was on Saturday nights many years ago that I and millions of others used to fine-tune our radios to pull the Opry across the mountains, to listen to Flatt and Scruggs and Webb Pierce and Roy Acuff and Minnie Pearl celebrate the country in us all. Now the Opryhouse is not where you go, and you don't get it on the radio. You go to Opryland, U.S.A., a theme park built by an insurance company. That is, you go if you want to. I don't.

But it was Saturday night, and I was in Nashville. So I asked around about where to hear Nashville music, and everybody seemed to agree on a certain section of downtown. It turned out to be the local porno district, which also maintained a few joints that promised live, authentic music. The one I visited also featured indigestible pizza, an outsized cover charge, and an acoustic guitarist whose contribution to the Nashville Sound that night was a medley of Peter, Paul, and Mary songs that even I could have sung. I headed back toward the motel room, reflecting on the notion that the town that calls itself "Music City, U.S.A," is the place where the music is manufactured, bought, sold, taped, mixed, packaged, and hyped, not necessarily the place where it may be heard and enjoyed. Then I managed to stumble across a church revival in a circus tent pitched on a vacant lot near downtown. They attracted people, including me, by blasting away with some delicious, live, suitably amplified rock music. I left when the music stopped and the proselytism started, but I gave them a dollar on the way out.

And on Sunday morning, while an impressive percentage of Nashville's population went to a more subdued church—mostly the Southern Baptist Church, of which Nashville is the Vatican—I drove out to Mount Juliet, a sort of countrified suburb, and I visited with Will Campbell.

Will is an ordained Baptist minister. He was born a little more than fifty years before in Amite County, Mississippi, to a family that Wilbur Cash would have described as yeoman farmers—a family with no history of slaveholding, and with no history of wealth, either. Will went to Yale Divinity School, but he never stopped being Southern. He was the pastor of a church in Bienville Parish, Louisiana, then the Director of Religious Life at the University of Mississippi, where there were a number of confrontations with those present and future state leaders who didn't share his Christian attitudes toward race relations. In one such case, someone literally placed a turd in a punchbowl at one of the university's religious functions. From 1956 until 1963 he worked with the National Council of Churches, traveling from one civil rights battleground to another, listening more than talking. He did not fit the minister's stereotype at all: Will usually carried his guitar, and he always chewed tobacco and cursed when he felt the situation would benefit from it, which in those days was pretty much all the time.

Will also was capable of, as they say, "taking a drink" from time to time, which led some observers in the hyper-hypocritical Southern religious community to conclude that he was an agent of Satan rather than of God. Since 1963 he has been the director and "preacher at large" of the Committee of Southern Churchmen, which has its headquarters in Nashville.

The day was hot enough to liquefy the tar on the highway, but Will and Brenda's little farm was cool and shaded and comfortable. Will showed me around the two acres they had planted (with food that they mostly give away), and he explained why he had mounted a gun rack in the rear window of his pickup truck ("It's to carry my walking sticks, and it also kind of helps when you're traveling in Mississippi, even if you don't have a gun"), and we stopped by the cool, breezy kitchen for some iced tea. Will took off his floppy old hat and eased himself into a chair. He wore old chino pants, a sweat-stained blue chambray work shirt, and properly scuffed pointy-toed Western boots.

I mentioned the trouble I had had in finding Nashville music, and Will picked up his guitar and sang a while. One of the songs, the one he wrote for his daughter when she got married a short time before, brought tears to my eyes. I had found the authentic music, not in Nashville on a Saturday night but in Mount Juliet on a Sunday noon hour, the church hour.

We walked back to Will's little homemade log-cabin office, and I asked him why, inasmuch as he was a Baptist preacher, he wasn't in church today.

"I *was* in church today," he replied. "I was in church when you and Brenda and I were sitting around the kitchen table drinking ice tea and singing country songs. You can't *go* to church. You can only *be* church."

Will is something of a critic of the organized, institutionalized church. It is his contention that when God's opponents discovered that crucifying him didn't work, they then attacked him from another direction: They institutionalized him. "And *that* has pretty much worked, it seems to me," said Will. The modern church, he added, has become "a franchise operation," a place of great power and enormous wealth and very little godliness.

"I don't accuse the institutional church of being bad," he said. "It's not bad. It's good. Every time there's a crisis somewhere, and people are counting up their quotas of allies, they say, 'Well, we've got the U.J.A., and we've got the Boy Scouts, and we've got the League of Women Voters, we've got the Red Cross, and we've got the church . . .'

"It's right up there with the rest of them. It's good. And God knows it's rich. So rich that if it should decide this morning at eleven o'clock to sell all of its holdings, we could solve the poverty problem in this country for a long time. And it's powerful. Very powerful. So powerful that if even a tenth of the people wearing the sign of the cross had decided that that war in Southeast Asia was unjust, it would have ended. The church is very powerful, very rich, and very good. But I don't see it as *the church.*"

Will Campbell has been called, by both those who were trying to compliment him and those who sought to condemn him, the "minister to the rednecks." By this they are referring to the time he has spent getting to know alienated, unprivileged white Southerners—in particular some from eastern North Carolina who were active in the Ku Klux Klan.

He shied away from this designation, when I mentioned it, as he shies away from most others. But it was true, he said, that his heritage had a lot to do with his particular interest in Southern whites. "Like a lot of other so-called white liberals," he said there in that log cabin, "I spent some time trying to deny my heritage and in looking for a home elsewhere, but I didn't find it. There was an awful lot of self-righteousness in a lot of us when we left home or were pushed from home when Momma or Daddy or Aunt Blanche or whoever didn't understand our newfound sophistication and enlightenment. But we didn't pull it off. None of us pulled it off." Will spat tobacco juice into a large barrel next to his roller-top desk.

He got interested in the forgotten Southerners, he said, for a couple of reasons. For one, the proponents of "Black Power" weren't at all wrong when, in the late sixties, they advised their white liberal colleagues in the movement to devote some energy to reforming members of their own race. For another, the sort of Southerners who end up in the Klan have really been victimized by their nation, their region, and their society.

Will has written about this in an article titled "The World of the Redneck," published in *Katallagete* ("be reconciled"), the journal of the Committee of Southern Churchmen. He wrote, in part, that "It is bad to have your back and your blood taken as happened to the Blacks. But there is a sense in which it is worse to have your *head* taken away. Through it all the Blacks knew what was happening, that they were suffering, and why, and who was causing it. And early in the game they set about the task of doing something about it. But we whites never got their head. The job on the redneck was more extensive because he had his *head* taken away. He still hasn't identified his 'enemy.' "

Will can explain, if he is asked, that he is not an apologist for the Klan. But neither does he hate such organizations. "They are not the most racist of groups," he said. "I have never asked anybody to get out of the Ku Klux Klan, any more than I ever asked anybody to resign his tenured position at a university—although I'm convinced that the university, as an institution, teaches, spawns, fosters and carries out more violence in one semester than the Ku Klux Klan has in its whole history. But I'm not defending the Klan any more than I would defend the Pentagon."

I told Will that I was trying, in this journey, to find out what was distinctive about the South, to determine which of the region's qualities should, and would, be saved. His reply was unexpectedly pessimistic—particularly coming as it did from a church person, and at the end of the churching hour, as hundreds of thousands of worshippers throughout the South were heading home, their stomachs growling and their minds lately filled with messages of optimism. Messages tempered, perhaps, with a threat or two of eternal damnation, Hollywood-style, but essentially messages of optimism.

"People used to talk of manners," said Will. "But more and more of that, of course, is disappearing. As are so many of the other qualities."

We listed, for each other, some of those other qualities: sense of family, sense of place, a feeling for the environment. Will said he was sorry, but that he felt they were in decline. "I think a lot of values, a lot of babies, got thrown out with the bath water," he said.

The bath water, of course, was the South's wrenching journey through the second liberation of its black citizens. Will had worked as hard as anyone to bring his native land through that traumatic, exhilarating experience. But, as he said, "We were so intent on correcting some of the injustices and inequities that we let some other things slip away from us." It was embarrassing to name some of those things, he said, because the words sounded so funny now: words like *honor,* and *integrity.*

"I guess the race thing is going to ultimately be our destruction," he said, after a long pause, a long searching for proper words. "The evil of it was so real that it *had* to be altered, had to be rooted out. And a lot of the virtues were simply associated with an evil system, and they died, too.

"And that's too bad, you know, if that is the price you've got to pay for a system that was evil. And the thing that makes it so tragic is that the South isn't any more guilty in that regard than anybody else."

Maybe less, I said, thinking of the shameful injustices of the North, made more shameful by all the hypocrisy surrounding them.

"Maybe less," said Will, and I felt myself catching his pessimism. The next morning I headed out, against Nash-

ville's Monday-morning commuter traffic, southwest toward Mississippi, where the evil of the system had so often
and so clearly manifested itself. For the the first time in
this journey I felt apprehension. Mississippi Fear, I used to
call it, back in the sixties.

III

Mississippi shadows and light

9

Eventually something changes

Secondary roads have minds of their own. *They* know where they're going, and they assume that the people traveling them know, too. If you're a stranger and you don't know, then you just have to slow down and adjust your speed, your pace, and your frame of mind to the curves and intersections, the grades and dips and bumps.

It seemed, that morning as I headed south out of Nashville toward Mississippi, that half the turtle population of Tennessee lived on the east side of the road and the other half lived on the west, and that each half had decided to pay visits to the other. I was constantly swerving to avoid them as they crossed the road. And I was constantly reminded, by the oily splats on the highways, that there are a lot of people who don't bother to swerve.

The countryside smelled good, although the sky was still thick and the forecasters were talking about a "stagnation advisory." But there was honeysuckle growing close to the road, and vines and roots and leaves, everything a deeper green now, late in May, a green maturing into summer. Every so often I crossed a stream with foliage on its banks so thick and lush that I couldn't see the water, but I knew it was opaque and brown and full of cottonmouths.

I went through towns so small that they weren't even on the map, and I passed places that had fun with the language, like the "One-Gallus Fox Hunter Camp." Even the unemotional title of a "Community Care Center" was softened, made more human, with the added words in regular, meaningful English: "Old Folks and Children Welcome."

The pressures to take the juice out of the language are about as heavy in the South as anywhere. The Natchez Trace Parkway, which the federal government is building roughly along the route of the old wilderness trail from Natchez to Nashville, is virtually nothing but nature with a thin ribbon of pavement running through it. But the National Park Service puts up signs saying "Nature Area, 1 Mile," and people exit there to see the nature for a few moments, and then they continue on down to the Picnic Area, and then to the Historical Area, and then maybe to the Recreational Area. All these Areas are planned and coordinated, of course, by the Bureaucratic Area.

And on the radio, an AM station that plays a lot of country and western and whose major advertisers sell feed and seed and fertilizer and pickup trucks, the man told me about my need to spray my fields with some of his marvelous pesticide. "Get in touch with your aerial applicator," he said, and I was shocked. I have known a few cropdusters in my time, men and one woman who flew those wonderful open-cockpit biplanes anytime, anywhere, and at any altitude, telephone lines or not, and I tried to imagine their responses to being referred to as "aerial applicators."

The going was slow, and I wondered if I were missing anything by not taking the interstates. My immediate answer to myself was no, missing nothing that shouldn't be missed. If I *had* gone on the interstates, I would have passed by a great deal: smells, sights, colors, shapes, and an incredible richness to the land that had not yet been lost. Will Campbell had been pessimistic about the disappearing qualities, and I suppose I was, too. But when you drive down an old highway like State 99 in Tennessee and see all those cows and dandelions, and fine old frame houses that have been carefully preserved, painted regularly and caulked and loved, that had people born in them and people die in them, and when you see that they have left the trees around the houses (for shade is very important in the South), when you see all that *continuity,* you have some hope. And when you pass a working farm—not an agribusiness place, not a corporate farm with its own logotype, but just a plain old farm that is operating and making a little money—then you have some hope, too.

All through the South, now, there are institutions of higher education that simply did not exist a few years ago. I passed one now: Columbia State College, a small institution with less than a dozen buildings, a neat line of poplars, carefully groomed lawns, a lot of athletic space; all of it across the highway from the Ponderosa Mobile Village. It all looked as if it had just appeared on the spot about six months before.

Most people don't use two hands to drive with here, because nobody's going all that fast and nothing too unexpected is going to happen. One hand is on the steering wheel, and the other rests in the window of the car or truck. When you meet someone on the highway, even if they are perfect strangers, you give them a little salute. The hand that is resting on the steering wheel raises a bit, and the fingers lift in a casual greeting, a hello.

There were lots of front porches in the little town of Hampshire, Tennessee. An elderly lady sat on one of them in a hard-backed chair, reading the Bible. She had grey hair and she wore one of those dresses that grandmothers sometimes wear—a dark fabric of purple-blue with little white dots. She said she had a case of the shingles and she was "taking a little sunbath."

The road cut briefly through northwesternmost Alabama, its four lanes proclaiming the relative wealth of that part of the state. And then, suddenly, without warning, the four lanes dissolved into two and I was in Mississippi, and I felt the old fear at the back of my neck. "Entering Tishomingo Co.," said the little green sign. Not "Welcome to Mississippi." No landscaped welcome stations with maps and brochures and ice water and clean restrooms.

The fear comes from the sixties, when I was a newspaper reporter, based first in Atlanta and later in New York, with the primary job of covering some of the civil rights movement in the South. There was, in those days, a lot of violence being directed by whites, some of them in official positions, against black people and their white sympathizers and, to a lesser but still painful extent, against reporters who came to witness and tell the rest of the world what was happening. I had received a small portion of that violence, and I had seen the effects of a lot more of it on others, and as a result there was a certain amount of fear that accompanied every trip into Mississippi.

Mixed in with all of this was a feeling that could only be called *guilt*. I was, in those days, in the minds of some of my acquaintances and even a few relatives, a turncoat Southern white. I believed in and wanted integration. The very nature of my work tended to promote integration. I think my news stories were fair and balanced, but my personal feelings were quite strong. I had no guilt over wanting integration. But I could not avoid the feeling that I had somehow betrayed a part of my heritage, that I had deliberately estranged myself from my very culture. And there was guilt over that, over the fact that I had not been able to make my friends understand the way I had taken.

I thought about all this now, ten years later, as I drove through Mississippi. I kept the speed well under fifty-five, for I wanted no brushes with deputy sheriffs. I kept my eyes on all three rear-view mirrors. I met several cars on the highway. Nobody waved as they had done in Tennessee.

There was a darkness about the place that had started as soon as I had crossed the state line: a darkness of environment and of the mind that troubled me as in the old days and that made the fear stronger in my neck. The roadsides were closer together here, the trees taller and wilder. The daylight was there, and it was bright, but less of it seemed to get to the ground. It was as dark as the inside of a tent. The light was lost, most of it, in Mississippi shadows.

The darkness, of course, was not all physical. Mississippi, or that portion of it that was allowed to vote, for decades had cursed itself with a series of political and educational leaders who had contributed to a worse darkness, the darkness of the mind.

Someone in an oncoming car waved a hello to me. I

passed a sign by a gas station. "Used Battries," it said, and I cheered up a little more.

I passed a funeral parlor that had been constructed out of two of the mobile homes that are transported on a truck and then bolted together. A pickup truck passed me, and standing in the back, looking intently at the world, was a fine-looking mule. And there was a sign pointing to a town named New Hope. And I passed my first mimosa tree.

Then the road took me to Booneville, and I stopped at a sporting goods and hardware store on the main highway. Jessie Campbell, who runs the place, saw the license plate and said something about my being a long way from home. I had been concerned about hauling that New York license through Mississippi, but Jessie Campbell was being pleasant about it. That started us talking.

The South, he said, was the right place to live. He'd been all over, including Oregon and Bermuda, when he had worked for the Air Force and for Monroe Calculators, and he'd decided to come back to Mississippi. "It's got a nice climate," he said, "and some of the finest small communities that you could ever see, and a long growing season, and very nice trees and grass, beautiful flowers.

"In other words, you have just about everything you need. And the living is easier. I think you have a way of life here that doesn't tend to be as fast as in some other places."

But what, I asked, about race? What about the preoccupation that had sapped Mississippi's energy for so long, poisoned its people so badly?

"It's almost nonexistent now," he said.

That was, I said, hard to believe. How could it have gone away?

"People realize now that it was wrong, and they've changed their ways. People—in Mississippi or anywhere—don't like to change, but when you see that something you've been doing is wrong, and when you get it pointed out to you the way we've had it pointed out to us, then eventually something changes."

In only a decade?

"Well, that's what I think happened. There's been a new generation of people, black and white, here. And there's been a pretty big rise in the standard of living of the black people. Plus, you've just got good people in the South. Better people than in the North, in my opinion."

Back on the road, heading for Tupelo and Jackson, I noticed that my neck was loosening up. Some of the tension was receding now, like the numbness of novocaine after a visit to the dentist's. Not all the fear was gone. I still was not sure I shared Jessie Campbell's optimism about the people of Mississippi, or of anyplace else. But the road didn't look as dark and dangerous as it had before.

Alvis Lassiter was drying a parachute on his large front lawn in Iuke, Mississippi, when I drove by, so I stopped to ask him why and to sneak in a question or two about the South. He had, he said, no special reason for having a parachute; he just liked the way it looked. As for the differences between the North and the South: "I can't explain it, but there *is* a difference. If you're born in the South, you're a Southerner, I guess. It's just like a red hog and a black hog."

In Tupelo I saw a bunch of young boys, in full uniform, playing football on a school athletic field. The warmth of a Mississippi May seemed out of place for football, but the boys went at it with autumn fury. About half of them were black and half were white, and there seemed to be no distinction between the colors. White and black girls stood and sat by the side of the field, watching and cheering and providing that age-old sexual boost to the boys on the field.

I asked at the motel for good places to find dinner, and I was disappointed when the clerk said the Sheraton Inn had the best food. I wanted Southern cooking, not another Bridgford Demi-Loaf. I collected my key and drove around to the room and started unloading my luggage. I noticed that a large young man in Wranglers and a white tee-shirt, who had been standing at the desk when I checked in, had followed me around. He parked his car several spaces away and left his wife, who was vastly pregnant, in it while he walked over to me. His Mississippi license plates contrasted with my bright orange advertisement for New York, and I grew a little apprehensive.

"I heard what you said back there," he said. "About looking for a place to, you know, *go* tonight. You interested in, say, some *hot* spots?"

I explained that I was just looking for a good place to eat. He smiled, just short of a leer, and I told him I meant eating dinner. He said in that case, he'd recommend the Sheraton Inn, too. I thanked him and he drove away.

The food was delicious at the Sheraton Inn, and for the first time in my life I ate catfish. It had not been frozen the previous year and run through a microwave oven. It was real, and so were the hushpuppies. The meal put a serious dent in my armor against franchise and chain operations.

Back on the Natchez Trace Parkway: the flagman on a road construction project was a beautiful young woman with a Farrah Fawcett-Majors hairdo. Then I passed an asphalt roller and a young woman was operating that, too. The flagman at the other end was a black man.

Patt Derian had told me, before she left Jackson to join the Carter administration in the State Department, that the capital of Mississippi had changed a lot. "Before," she had said, "everybody was entirely absorbed, socially and intellectually, with the struggle that was centered around race. As tensions have subsided between people, it's been kind of like *springtime*. People are relaxed enough now to think truly about the quality of their lives."

To paraphrase Will Campbell's comment into a pulp, with the changing of the bath water had come a slightly different baby. As Jackson grew and changed and got rid of some of its repressive politicians and the more reprehensible elements of the media, it also became the embryo of a franchised operation. It was becoming a little Atlanta, with interstates carrying ever-increasing burdens of traffic long before and after the normal rush hours, a constant slither of merges and exits, alongside of which were most of the fast-food outfits and all the major motels; shopping centers next to more shopping centers, all of it flying past at fifty-seven or so miles an hour, the official speed by which life is lived and measured in a growing urban center.

Jackson was a constant string of A & P's Open 24 Hours, Master Hosts, Kentucky Fried Chicken (the Colonel's portrait getting smaller and smaller now, as the operation becomes more conglomerated), Bonanza steak joints, International Houses of Pancakes, Package Liquor Sold Here (in Mississippi you used to have to buy it from a bootlegger), McDonald's 20 Billion Sold (elsewhere I had seen 21 and 24 billion), the Standard Be-Bop Record Shop, Tire Sale, Baskin-Robbins Have You Had Your Ice Cream Today, Free Car Wash With Fillup. On the radio the local gas monopoly urged people to buy gas-powered outdoor grills, and they coped with the fuel-crisis issue by saying that energy wisely used is energy saved.

I supposed, as I floated through it all, that the people of Jackson could probably survive it. If they could live through the Civil War and the civil rights movement, they could live through this.

Then I pulled a cop over. My great fear upon entering Mississippi a day earlier had been that a cop would pull me over. But now it was different. I asked H. E. Butler if he would stop and talk for a minute because he was the first black policeman I had ever seen in that state. H. E. Butler was a sergeant in the Jackson Police Department.

"Yes, things have changed," he said, and just then a dark green pickup truck squealed to a halt and a tall black man in a different uniform got out. He wanted to know if Butler were in any trouble.

The tall man was J. T. Watkins, a conservation officer for the Mississippi Game and Fish Commission, which used to be just another part of the state's official structure of racism. Watkins wore a couple of badges, one of which testified that he was a karate instructor.

"I'm the first black conservation officer," he said, once it was established that Sergeant Butler was in no danger. "But I won't be the last. Things are opening up. The people in Mississippi are more gentle than the people in the rest of the country think." It was clear that when he said "the people in Mississippi," he meant *all* the people in Mississippi.

10

A reclamation of human life

I went to lunch with Kenneth Dean and Jack Breed in Jackson. Dean is a liberal Democrat, a Baptist minister, a white, and a native of Maryville, Tennessee. From 1964 until 1970 he was the director of the Mississippi Council on Human Relations. Then he joined an interracial group that successfully challenged the license of television station WLBT-TV on the grounds that it had inadequately served the black community. He served as the president of the station until early in 1977, when he became the pastor of a church in Memphis.

Jack Breed is a not-so-liberal Republican, a native of Poplarville, Mississippi, now a resident of Jackson; a businessman with interests in an armed guard company, hardware, and a manufacturers' representatives firm. Dean invited Breed to the lunch, he explained, so that I might get a more balanced view of things. This is a quality I have noticed before in many of my fellow Southerners and not at all in Northerners: a desire by them to test themselves and their most deeply-held convictions on the ancient Southern field of informal debate; and, perhaps as importantly, to maintain their ties to those who disagree with them.

The food, in a restaurant a block or so from the television station, was good and simple and home-style, and the iced tea was real. I asked Breed and Dean if it were correct, as I had been told several times and as I was beginning to see with my own eyes, that Mississippi had changed. Yes, they said, it had. I told them what Jessie Campbell had said the day before in Booneville: that whites had realized they had been wrong in their attitudes toward blacks, and that they had therefore changed. Could it possibly be that simple and straightforward?

"I think there are several factors that I see leading to change in Mississippi and in the South in general," said Dean. "Number one, I've worked for some fifteen years in race relations, and I don't know of any instances in which change has taken place except that it was brought about by legal action. I don't know of any bunch of whites who got together and said, 'This thing is wrong; let's initiate a change and do it because it's right.' A *lot* of them sat down and did that *after* legal action was brought. They said, 'It's wrong to continue as we are, because we'll get in trouble with the government if we don't change.' "

The second factor, he said, was the passage of more advanced federal wage legislation, which set a higher minimum and which included more categories of workers. "This began to put some change in poor people's pockets," he said. "And this caused a change in attitude on the part of the small merchant. He no longer saw Joe as 'a poor nigger.' Joe was now a paying customer. It effected a new level of dignity."

The third factor was the broadening of the federal food

stamp program. It, too, gave blacks some bargaining power in a grocery store. "The fourth thing that I think has been important," he said, "is voter registration projects. They have given blacks political power, so you've now got politicians who are no longer talking bad about blacks. Instead, they're saying, 'We got to reckon with them.'

"And I think the fifth issue, which encompasses all of those first four in varying degrees, has been the success of the federal, and in some instances state, programs that have allowed for local community organization." Dean had been working on a study, sponsored by the Field Foundation, which seeks to compare the problems of hunger and malnutrition among Mississippi black children now with the situation a decade ago. Back then, the Head Start pre-school program was violently opposed by white Mississippi politicians, who saw it (correctly) as a device by which powerless blacks and poor whites might organize themselves and do something about their miserable living conditions.

The ten-year survey, which at the time I visited Dean had not yet been completed, was revealing great improvements in the health of black children who had been exposed to Head Start and food stamps. "These programs," said Dean, "have produced a more healthy young black child and more healthy young black adults, which allows them to learn better, to work more, to take care of themselves, to compete and cope better in society. Plus these programs have tended, in most communities, to develop a local, indigenous black leadership, which is important.

"So I think things have changed in Mississippi. The element of fear seems to be gone." There were still forces at work, he said, to keep the state in the category of what Ole Miss historian James Silver once called, in a 1963 speech to his colleagues, "the closed society." "But," said Dean, "Mississippi has changed."

There were, however, significant pockets of resistance to all this change, in Mississippi and in the rest of the South. The opposition no longer came so much from the deputy sheriffs and courthouse hangers-on and the small town merchants who rode with guns at night. Many of these, said Dean, had been imprisoned or harassed into silence and inactivity by the Federal Bureau of Investigation.

Rather, he said, the most serious resistance to change in Mississippi came from the church and from the education establishment. "These are the two institutions that have tried to maintain a closed society," he said. "They have submitted to openness to a lesser degree than other forces operating in society." Nowhere has the resistance been more manifest than in the creation—by representatives of many of the organized religious groups in the South—of private academies, known to their critics as "seg academies." The institution of public education, which had had almost a quarter of a century to get accustomed to the idea of school desegregation, and which hadn't done a very good job of it, had in many places become re-segregated as the academies had siphoned off white children.

"The academies mean you have a dual school system," said Dean, "and you tend to develop parallel curricula. You tend to have two different philosophies of history being taught. You're not, for instance, going to have the academies talking in their history classes about the contribution of blacks to America. You're going to have them essentially fostering what I would call a right-wing, racist orientation to education. They really are not preparing people to live together. So, while we are, on some fronts, making a great deal of change, these institutions are still trying to maintain the closed society. And this is important, because the two major social institutions in the South are the church and the school."

We talked a while about the qualities of the South that

ought to be preserved. One characteristic of the region that should be discarded as quickly as possible, said Dean, was ignorance. "Any of the romantic aspects of the South that people would want to maintain," he said, "if they're related to maintaining that ignorance, then I'm against it. I'm willing to give up some of those old, romantic ideas and thoughts and customs of the South if it means that they stand in the way of people becoming better educated."

Some have said the Southerner has a better-developed sense of family than does his or her non-Southern neighbor. Dean, who has done family counseling in the North and South, disagrees. He does concur with the widespread idea that the Southerner is closer to religion. "But religion in the South is the last stronghold of resistance to change," he said, "so I don't see religion in the South as being a value that needs to be maintained. In fact, I would say that's the first orientation that needs to be changed—our relationship to religion."

The region's environment is of major importance. "The greatness of the South," said Dean, "lies in its ability, in terms of climate and geography, to produce food. I think that in the future, the balance of power in the world is going to lie between the oil-producing countries and the food-producing countries. And as the oil diminishes, I think the importance of food production becomes far more important. The South has the climate, it has the soil, it has the know-how. One thing that we're *not* lacking in the South is agricultural education.

"And there's another part of the culture that I think is worth preserving. I think there's a stronger emphasis in the South on the worth of the individual. I realize that this has been isolated for white people, not for blacks. But I think it's a virtue that's worth maintaining: the belief that the individual has dignity; that no matter what his station in life, he has a right to his work, to his relationship with the land, a right to become free, to maintain himself."

So, I asked him, you're optimistic?

"I'm very encouraged," he replied. "I started working in Mississippi in sixty-four, and it was a tough time. There was a lot of fear. And now I think there's been a lot of change. It did me good to go back and look at black children in the Delta a few weeks ago and see that, rather than being anemic and lethargic and having swollen bellies and being small in stature, the children are more nearly normal. They relate to you and play with you, and they can say 'Yes' and 'No.' They can express themselves and they can learn. To see the reclamation of human life like that is a very beautiful thing."

The waitress brought us some more iced tea, and she smiled pleasantly at us all, and we smiled back. For the first time in a long while, I was feeling good about Mississippi. Jack Breed broke his silence.

"I think a lot of people have gone in for overkill in this thing," he said. "And I think what good that's been accomplished could be wiped out if we're not careful." I asked him what he meant.

"It's reverse discrimination," he said. "A young white man, working for a big company, can't get a promotion based on his ability. He can't get a job or a promotion, because he isn't black. Federal, state, whatever. The best example I know of is the telephone company. The kids are being persecuted because they're white. Now, this doesn't undo any wrong that's been done in the past. Equality is one thing; an unfair advantage is another. . . . The doors were locked. They were opened. They *should* have been opened. But they ought not to be locked on somebody else now."

It was not the first time on this journey I had heard this complaint. It is a widespread one among whites who are neither ultra-conservatives nor overt racists. I would not be surprised if it eventually assumed major importance, unless someone in a position to give us leadership articulates the need for blacks to be allowed to catch up. It is not necessarily a matter of "reverse discrimination." It is as simple as acknowledging that, in so much of American life, we have had a black quota of zero for hundreds of years, and that it won't destroy us to establish a different quota for a few years longer. "Compensation" was the word Ken Dean used at lunch that day, softly but firmly.

Dean had some practical experience with compensation at his television station. When his organization, Communications Improvement, took over WLBT, it immediately instituted a policy that no more whites would be hired until blacks had achieved occupational equity. "We found," he said, "that you couldn't integrate a television station—and I don't think you can integrate any institution or agency—unless you begin integration from the top down.

"Most people try to integrate from the bottom up, and what that means is that everybody there views each new black employee in the light of a janitor because everybody is keying everything from a janitor position to a clerk position to some other, higher, middle-range position. So you're trying to build from janitor up. So we hired a black general manager. We found that a white general manager, every time a job would open up, would give us a rationale as to why he had to hire a white. It didn't matter what the job was. If it was a receptionist—which actually happened—he said it has to be a white because she's meeting the public. If it was a technician, he said it has to be white because there are no experienced black ones."

How familiar the words sounded. I've heard it all over the North. We really want to hire *them,* but we can't find any qualified *ones.* The words *them* and *ones* sound suspiciously like *niggers.*

"What we found out when we hired a black general manager," continued Dean, "was that we had good applicants from the black community because they believed that we *wanted* black applicants. Almost overnight, so to speak, we were able to realize our integration of forty percent of this television station, because we had integrated from the top down. I don't know of anybody else in the United States of America who's willing to follow that pattern, of integrating from the top down. And I think it's absolutely important.

"Five of our ten top executives in this TV station are black. And the beautiful part of it is that the community has accepted it; they've endorsed it; the ratings of this station are the highest they've ever been; the income is the highest it's ever been." And it happened in Jackson, Mississippi.

We finished the delicious meal and the waitress thanked us for coming. We wandered back to the television station for more talking. When we got there Ken Dean asked me to turn on my tape recorder because he wanted to say something he thought might interest me. I turned it on.

"In Jackson, historically speaking," he said, "one of the last places of public accommodations to continue to refuse blacks, or whites with long hair or beards, is the restaurant in which you just ate. I took us over there to see if they'd turn us away. You're the first time that I know of that they'd let a man with a beard eat there. So maybe things are opening up a little bit in Jackson, Mississippi."

11

Homecoming

A number of thoughtful Southerners have arrived in recent years at a conclusion about their homeland that sounds, when you think about it for more than a moment, like an eternal verity of the first order. The Southerner is a member of an *ethnic group,* they have declared, or might as well be. The Southerner's feeling of identity with his and her peers is not all that different from the feelings of Italian-Americans for theirs, or Irish-Americans, or Polish-Americans, or any of the other racial, religious, or national groups of the sorts that are somewhat crassly referred to, especially by big-city politicians at election-time, as "ethnics."

Two persons in the academic world who have paid attention to the Southerner's ethnicity may be found in the same building, but in different departments, in Chapel Hill. George Brown Tindall is a distinguished professor of history, mostly Southern history, at the University of North Carolina. He has written several books on the South, the latest one, published in 1976 by the Louisiana State University Press, being a collection of essays entitled *The Ethnic Southerners*. In it, he confronts the problem raised time and again by those (particularly fancy Northern writers) who visit the South, see the ruins of the small farms and the clutter of the cities and the shopping centers, and then pronounce the region totally Americanized. "The South *has* changed," Tindall told me earlier in the trip, "but the process of change doesn't necessarily mean the South is losing its distinctiveness. Some of these things [we had been talking about interstates and fast-food joints] may not run as deep as one thinks." And in his book he reminds us: " . . . whatever the future may hold, the South has repeatedly displayed a striking knack for accepting change without losing the sense of its separate identity."

John Shelton Reed has an office down the hall and stairs from Tindall's. He has approached the question of the South's identity from the viewpoint of a sociologist, and, more importantly for those of us in the laity, from the viewpoint of a social scientist who can still write and speak English, and who even has a sense of humor. His book, *The Enduring South*, published in 1974 by the University of North Carolina Press, also cautions against the notion that the South's distinguishing characteristics are disappearing.

In that book, Reed used the information that was available to measure Southerners' feelings in three major areas that frequently have been listed as peculiarly Southern: localism, or "attachment to place"; a more positive, accepting attitude toward violence and the use of force; and a deeper commitment to religion. He found, and presented in his book in a highly readable manner, evidence that these three factors *are* more intense in the South than most anywhere else.

We had talked a while, back in the early spring, about the Southerner's attachment to place, and about how the trend for many years was for upwardly-mobile Southerners to flee the region—to become exiles, as I had done and as Reed, a Tennessean who went to school at Harvard and Columbia, had done.

"That may have changed," he said, "now that you can get jobs around here. That's why everybody moved, you know—to go away and get jobs. It's only been in the last decade that there have been more people coming into the South than there were going out. And an interesting thing that a demographer friend told me was that a very large proportion of those in-migrants are *return* migrants— Southerners who had left and who are now coming back."

Hugh Jackson stood behind the counter, sheltered by air conditioning from the Gulf-coast heat and humidity, and he talked about how great Mississippi is. He had moved there, he said, for the same reasons that thousands of others do who are heading for the Sunbelt states, and particularly for the Southern Sunbelt states. The reasons are varied, but they all seem to add up to something vaguely known as the "quality of life." For Hugh Jackson, it was important that his two children grow up in what he called a "decent environment," and that's why he and his family moved to Gulfport from New York City in the fall of 1976.

All of this is not very unusual or surprising. Nor is it surprising that Hugh Jackson is a native Southerner, one of those who has returned to his homeland. What makes things a little different is the fact that Hugh Jackson is black.

Jackson works in a local retail branch of a national electronics chain, in a shopping center along the strand between Gulfport and Biloxi. At the time of our discussion he was thirty-six years old, articulate, with a quick sense of humor. He is what the ad agencies call "upwardly mobile," an example of a black person who is making it in this world, a person who wants some of the finer things of life and who can afford to pay for a few of them. He is also an example of another sort of American: the black who is heading South to live.

Less than a generation ago, as John Shelton Reed had pointed out, Southerners were leaving their region in droves. Many were blacks, and many went to the cities of the Middle Atlantic and Northeastern states in search of more nearly equal opportunities in employment, housing and everything else. The North was sometimes called "Freedomland" by Southern blacks; it was a place described and redescribed by relatives home for the holidays until it had taken on mythical aspects that rivalled those of the Southland; it was a place that had become, in the telling, not too unlike the scenes of the Life Everlasting that were painted on Sunday mornings in powerful, lovely cadences by black Southern preachers.

There was, of course, a certain amount of truth in these reports, but it is likely that there was also a good deal of embroidery. Nobody wants to admit that an important decision he or she has made (and what could be more important than deciding to leave one's homeland?) was a mistake. And it was definitely true that there were jobs in Freedomland that simply did not exist for blacks in the South.

So a lot of blacks moved to the North, where they were confined to ghettoes owned by white realtors and managed by white politicians with the connivance of a few apostate black "leaders." In some cases the migrants and their issue filled whole cities, such as Newark and Detroit, and then the realtors and politicians abandoned them altogether.

Those migration patterns, for both whites and blacks, have changed dramatically. Now the South is increasing in population. A recent report by E. Evan Brunson and Thomas D. Bever for the Southern Growth Policies Board notes that, of the 11.3 million population increase in the entire United States since 1970, some fifty-three percent occurred in the South (which they defined as fifteen states). The great majority of migrants to the South were and are white, but now black in-migration is taking place for the first time. More recent figures in a 1978 Census Bureau document show, meantime, that blacks are accelerating their departures from the Northeastern states. From 1960 until 1970, said the report, the nine Northeastern states had a net gain of 612,000 blacks, most of whom came from the South. The pattern changed from 1970 to 1975, when there was a net *loss* of 64,000 blacks. And in the shorter period from 1975 until 1977, the net Northeastern loss rose to 104,000. "This has to be a reflection of expanding employment opportunities in the South and declining opportunities in the North," said Larry H. Long, an author of the report, in a newspaper story.

Perhaps Freedomland has lost some of its luster.

"New York City almost made a racist out of me," said Hugh Jackson. "I lived there for seventeen years. When you compare New York, or any Eastern city, with Mississippi, you find a kind of subtle bigotry there that doesn't exist in the South. And it was having an effect on me. That's one reason I came back."

Jackson was born in Alabama. His family moved to Perry County, Mississippi, when he was less than a year old. He went to segregated schools, the last of which was Mississippi Valley State College. As soon as he was able, he left the South for New York City. That was in September of 1959. There he married a Mississippi woman, became a father, and found a home in the borough of Queens. He became a manager for a finance agency, and later sold real estate, which remains as one of New York's more segregated institutions.

He enjoyed New York, in a way. It is difficult not to, in a way. But he also saw that Freedomland (and Jackson emphasized that he was using New York as an example of the entire North) had its flaws. "There's more of everything there," he said. "There are more jobs; there are better jobs. But there's also more hatred, more racism.

"Everybody in New York lives in their own world. And the black man in New York is still the low man on the totem pole. New York is terribly ethnic-oriented. They have the Irish, and they have the Jews, and they have the Italians, and they have a few other groups, and among all these groups the black man is the last one that's given any consideration."

But in the South, I said, there had been two groups, and one of *them* had kept the other down, too.

"Right," he said. "And that hasn't necessarily changed all that much. But there seems to be more of a willingness on the part of Southerners to admit that there's a problem and to take some constructive steps toward trying to alleviate it."

Gradually, through his years in New York, Jackson discovered that the Northern environment was not the one for him, and surely not the one for his children. "I got into some fairly serious arguments with the blacks up there," he said, "because there are still a lot of blacks who think the East *is* the promised land." Friends would express their outrage at the murder of a young black Mississippian, and Jackson would remind them of the more recent killing of a black youth in New York City by the police.

"There was a kind of a meeting point," he said that afternoon in Gulfport. "New York was getting worse, and the South was getting better. One was moving backward while the other was moving in a more positive direction."

And now? Hugh Jackson had been back in Mississippi since September, 1976. Had he made the right choice?

"Let me tell you something," he said. "I would raise eyebrows if I had lived under the same conditions in New York as I live under in Mississippi. I live in an apartment complex over here on the beach. We are—and it's strictly by chance—the only black family in there. And it's wonderful. And if I have encountered any kind of hostility, or anything but a super-genuine attitude, I wish God would destroy me.

"I'll tell you what happened: I was moving in. I backed the trailer in to unload. My neighbors—they were all white, and nobody knew me—suddenly appeared to help. Before I could unhitch the trailer, there were four guys downstairs to help me unload. And this wasn't rehearsed."

Why, I asked, did he think they had done that?

"Because they're genuine," he said, without hesitation. "Southerners are more genuine than other people. Now, I'll tell you something else: in the next five minutes, if they had gotten angry, they might have called me a nigger. And if I had gotten angry back at them, I might have called them honkies. That's not what happened, but it *could* have happened. You see, there's something very basic to the Southerner that is not basic in the North. You just know where you stand all the time."

And his children. He was happy that his children now would grow up in an environment where they would know where they stood. Hugh Jackson said it wouldn't even bother him if they went to all-black schools. What was important was that their learning, and their lives, and their relationships with other people be *genuine*.

Was there any likelihood, I asked him, that his children *would* go to all-black schools?

"No," he said with a smile. "There are no segregated public schools in Mississippi anymore."

12

Souvenirs of Mississippi

It was real summer now, in the South and else-where. The secondary roads are always more interesting, but they were even more so now. It looked as if everybody in the Southern half of rural America had erected a road-side stand and was selling corn that had been picked that morning, beans and peaches and deep crimson tomatoes, ready for slicing that night and not a moment later.

I stopped at one of the stands to get some peanuts. The youth who was running it had red hair and a face full of freckles, and he was in his early teens. He said, as many had said when they saw the license plates, "Wherebouts in New York you *from*?"

Brooklyn, I said.

"You're not from the *Bronx,* huh?"

No, I said, Brooklyn. Do you know somebody from the Bronx?

"No," he said, "but I heard about it, and I heard it was pretty rough up there."

I thought, as I drove off eating my peanuts, that there were a lot of people in the Bronx who had heard that Mississippi was pretty rough, too.

There was another side to the summer. Much of the land had been parched like one of those peanuts by the drought. You could see it in those unfortunate places, in the ruined corn stalks and the yellowed underleaves of the tobacco plants, even in the little personal gardens by the sides of houses, their tomato plants wilted and their turnips lifeless.

Drought is a difficult thing to pin down. People's work, their planning, their investments were being destroyed. You knew that because you read it in the paper and heard it on the news. But you did not see people walking around as in Hollywood movies, their eyes glazed by destitution. The Red Cross did not come with blankets and cots, as after a flood. And yet people you talked to at the country crossroads and filling stations spoke of being "wiped out." The men squatted effortlessly in classic rural fashion and sketched simple designs in the dust and squinted at the sun.

That night a thunderstorm came. The noise enveloped the county, five counties, half a state, and the flashes shook the ground and the rain was torrential, if brief. It washed some of the red dust off your car and lowered the temperature. The next day the television news said the new front had brought a period of cooler air, and that meant a good weekend coming up for boaters and swimmers and fishers. But at the country crossroads and filling stations the farmers pushed back their baseball-type caps with advertisements for tractors and spark plugs on them and spoke of how it was "only half a nickel's worth" of rain, and of how the drought continues.

You sensed from all this that a disaster was in the making this summer, just as the previous winter's record cold and snow had been disastrous for some people. But drought is a difficult thing to pin down. It comes slowly and without much drama, unlike the floods of Pennsylvania and Colorado, and it stays a long time; and it is possible to pretend to ignore it completely if you have a nice, non-agricultural job in the city and do not spend too much time at country crossroads and filling stations.

The crawfish of southeastern Louisiana suffered from the winter's cold, but the Cajuns made sure there'd be enough around for the summer. The Cajuns love crawfish so much they probably *willed* the little creatures to grow and breed.

I had breakfast at Broussard Brothers' restaurant in Gulfport, Mississippi, which is not quite as much Cajun country as Louisiana, but which comes close. In the middle of the table was the biggest bottle of Tabasco sauce I have ever seen. Every person connected with the place, most of whom were named Broussard, was, shall we say, clearly not suffering from underweight. I share in that same general lack of skinniness, and I guess that as I looked around the room my thought was written all over my face, for the waitress said, voluntarily: "We're *all* pretty good advertisements for our restaurant."

Then she brought me the standard, simple breakfast: grits, sausage, fried eggs on top of rice, coffee, a delicious pastry. There were about two pounds of food there, most of it carbohydrates. She watched me explore the plate—I had never before even thought of fried eggs on rice—and commented: "It *is* a filling meal."

A local guide to what's happening in Biloxi—one of those semi-literate booklets you find in your motel room next to the Bible—listed one Camille Foret and his alias, the Crawfish King, under "Eating," and I went in search of the gentleman. It turned out that Foret is in the business of cooking large quantities of shrimp, crabs, and especially crawfish for parties, conventions, and similar gatherings. He doesn't have a restaurant, although I would be there on opening night if he ever started one.

Until such time as that happens, he sends hungry individuals to the place of his cousin, Frenchie Bourgeois, down the road in Ocean Springs, where they can eat themselves silly with such delicacies as marinated crab claws and stuffed eggplant. As for himself, Camille Foret is in what you might call the volume crawfish business.

I saw him early one morning. Late the night before he had driven one hundred eighty-five miles into Louisiana, bought eight hundred pounds of live crawfish, driven back, drunk two shots of whiskey, slept a couple hours, and then got up at four A.M. to start cooking them in his huge pot. He had a rush order to cater a small convention. You figure about sixteen pounds of meat from each one hundred pounds of crawfish.

"This is Cajun cooking," said Foret. "Best cooking in the world. Makes you a better lover." The small, cinder-block room behind the grocery store was filled with the incredibly good smell of cooking crawfish. Those that hadn't yet been cooked were crawling all over the place, pinching Foret through his rubber gloves and obviously looking for the way back to Louisiana. When they came out of the cooker they were bright red, like miniature lobsters.

"Sit down," said Foret. "Sorry I don't have a chair." He motioned toward a tall fiber drum that was the right height for sitting. Stenciled on its side was the legend, "Cayenne Pepper 100 Lbs."

"We use a lot of cayenne in our cooking," he said. His face, now that I noticed it, was the color of the hot pepper. He handed me a crawfish. I snapped it open and sucked out the meat and juices. It was even better than fried eggs on rice.

"When I finish the crawfish, they want a hundred pounds of potatoes." He pointed to two sacks of small, red-skinned potatoes. "They specifically asked me to cook the potatoes in the same water the crawfish were in, like I did last year. It gives them that spicy seafood taste."

It used to be, he said, that Cajuns were about the only people who liked to eat crawfish. "But that's changing now," he said. "In the past two or three years we've been shipping them all the way up to Maine. People are learning that crawfish is something better than just bait. People are coming *here* to eat it, too, I mean, people are moving to the South. Moving here from the North, mostly the Northeast. And when they do come here, they learn to eat our food.

"As a matter of fact, they learn to do lots of things that we Southerners do. They fit right in. It surprised me at first. They don't have any problem whatsoever fitting in, because they're our type of people."

I realized that I had heard Southerners make that point before: not that other Americans were moving to the South—that's a well-known trend—but that the migrants seemed not only willing but eager to accommodate themselves to "the Southern way of life," whatever that is. They slow down, become apparently more relaxed, start eating crawfish and asking for grits in restaurants.

Could it be that the rest of the population, which has looked down upon the South for all these years, now wants to become Southern?

I was leaving Mississippi now, amazed at the changes I had seen. The old tension in the back of the neck, the old fears that had been with me when I entered the state—these had gone. What had been the state's profound obsession with race seemed to have vanished.

Racism had not disappeared, of course. Deep in the impoverished Delta, it was being practiced daily, and I knew that if I looked around a little in Jackson or Biloxi or Tupelo or anyplace else I would find it. But as a *relative thing*, Mississippi had changed. I encountered, and felt, and smelled, and sensed, far less racism there than I did on an ordinary day in Freedomland. And, more importantly, I think, I sensed a feeling of something approaching *joy* among black Mississippians, a joy that came from knowing that finally they had the strength they needed in order to live with some semblance of happiness. For all those years they went to those hot, steamy mass meetings and they sang those Movement songs: "Ain't gonna let _____ _____ put me down, put me down, put me down. . . ." (You filled in the blanks with the name of the local bigot—Bull Connor, George Wallace, the police chief.) And now the people of the Movement had won. They had not been put down. The result, for a tiny few of them, was the cultivation and fruition of a lifelong hatred against the whites, all whites, who had tried to put them down. But for most, I think, it has been a kind of a joy.

A black police woman was directing traffic in Biloxi, and I slowed down in the intersection to ask her if this were the way to Lee Street. "Right ON, baby!" she shouted back, with a great big smile, and I found myself saying "all-RIGHT" in return.

A local radio station broadcast a news item about the governor of Mississippi going to a fund-raising event for President Carter, and added that "other state Democratic leaders may join him." One of the leaders mentioned was Aaron Henry, a black man who heads the National Association for the Advancement of Colored People in Mississippi and who is one of the most courageous black leaders in the South. The radio station made no mention of Henry's race.

Not long afterward, Aaron Henry sent a letter to his colleagues in the Movement, asking that they act charitably toward United States Senator James O. Eastland, who for decades had been one of the nation's top-ranked racists. Wrote Henry: "If we, the members of the black community, give him a chance, he will perform in a manner in the future that will come close to, if not altogether, a complete reversal of his negative actions of the past."

I walked along the sandy beach at Biloxi. In a souvenir shop I looked at the sew-on and stick-on patches—it is with patches and tee-shirts that we seem most capable of expressing ourselves these days—and I saw all the usual ones that are based on Farrah Fawcett-Majors and on citizens' band radio. Then there was one that had a comic rendition of a bewhiskered old codger and the Confederate battle flag and the words, "Surrender Like Hell." And beside that, in the black, green, and red colors that have come to symbolize Afro-American consciousness, the slogan, "Black Is Beautiful." And beside that, one that said, "Mississippi I Love You." All side by side.

I walked the beach, which I always do when I have a chance. It was not too crowded, and several people voluntarily greeted me as I walked by. Friendly people. The Mississippi license plates say "The Hospitality State." Of the maybe one hundred couples I saw in my walk, two were interracial. Mississippi has changed. The South has changed.

And Alabama. I stopped at the official welcome center, as I always do, because I am a nut about maps. This center, like many in the South, was bordering on the luxurious. It was full of modernistic symbol-signs (bent arrows with red slashes through them instead of "No Left Turn") and dog-walking trails and wheelchair ramps and proclamations about No Overnight Parking, and Security Guard on Duty, and live oaks, and new buildings that would not look out of place on a university campus.

And there were two water fountains, a sight that rang bells from a South of long ago. But then you looked closer and saw that one of them was closer to the ground than the other. It was for children and other little people.

And Florida. At the welcome center there, on the other side of Mobile, they asked you if you would like some complimentary fruit juice. It turned out to be *grape*fruit juice. I wondered if the state were embarrassed about Anita Bryant, the singer and TV commercial hustler for the state's orange-squeezers who at that time was also crusading against homosexuals. I doubt if they were offering grapefruit juice for that reason, but it would have been nice if they were.

I set up my tent, with great trepidations, in a national seashore campground on Santa Rosa Island in westernmost Florida. The trepidations were there because I dislike cheek-by-jowl camping; I am a backpacker by nature and I think you go into the woods for peace and quiet and meditation and learning about nature and yourself, not to run your air conditioner and play with your color TV. The ranger didn't help matters much when he replied to my question about how to get to the beach by saying that it was "quite some distance—about a quarter of a mile."

But the apprehension soon diminished. My neighbors were polite and quiet and I was in a section with no electricity, which took care of the TV-and-air-conditioner situation and which made it easier to converse with the skunk who came sniffing around at night and with the raccoon who perched in the live oak overhead.

But late one night I heard music from across the way. I was prepared to be angry about it, but there was something different about this music. It was live. Somehow that made it more tolerable. I wandered over and Danny, the fellow who was playing the lead guitar, invited me to sit down and have some wine. They were playing folk songs and mellow early Beatles and an occasional Gram Parsons. Danny was chugging copiously from a gallon bottle of wine of awful lineage. A young woman named Ruth, who had a voice that almost sounded like Joan Baez and Judy Collins together, was singing. Another young man, who kept quiet and drank little wine, was playing another guitar. The only light was from a dying wood fire in the middle of the circle. You could see only the vague outlines of people's faces.

Ruth said she was from Ocean Springs, Mississippi, and that she was camping in a tent nearby. She, too, had heard the music and come over to sing. Danny said he was from Gadsden, Alabama, and that he was the leader of the group.

"We play mostly Ramada Inns in the South," he said, and I must say he didn't sound overly enthusiastic about it. "We sort of, uh, find ourselves at liberty for the next three weeks, by which I mean we don't have any work. And we're a little, uh, short of cash, so we decided to come to the woods for a while." The band was living in a couple of tents, sleeping all day and playing all night. It was obvious from the debris around them that they had been there for some time.

Danny said they did *not* play folk and early Beatles at the Ramada Inns, but rather imitations of horrid popular songs that the patrons demanded. He named some, and I was happy to notice that I didn't recognize them. He said that the group's first three songs of an evening, during those evenings when they were working, were designed to see what kind of music the audience wanted. "It's pretty atrocious stuff," he said. "Not like what we're doing tonight."

Between songs, you could hear the surf rolling against the beach a quarter mile away.

A van with Virginia license plates pulled up in the parking space across from mine late the next morning and a young man started preparing a meal. He said he had just gotten out of the army—he had been an enlisted man, stationed at the Pentagon—and he was on his way to Louisiana to get married. "I'm just taking my time, going across the South, stopping when I feel like it," he said. "I'm not due in Shreveport for another week. This'll be the last time I'm on my own, so I'm just taking it easy."

He was from the state of Washington. I asked about his impressions of the South. He thought a long time before he answered. His wife-to-be, he said, was a Southerner, and he knew she and her family were nice. And he had known some decent Southerners in the army. "But I was prepared, you know, for more of the standard redneck thing, and I haven't found much of that. People have

been incredibly friendly to me down here. I was surprised
at it: the friendliness of the Southern people. It's not what
I was led to expect at all."

Susan Dubose and Bill Bullard were from Andalusia,
Alabama; a nice young couple. They occupied the camp-
site next to mine. She worked for a firm that sold automobile parts, and he made custom hunting knives for
collectors and others who appreciate such things. He also
was a member of a band that played on weekends at
places like VFW and American Legion clubs. He had
heard the music from Danny's group, but he hadn't wandered over; "I hear too much music as it is," he explained.

They were good and friendly neighbors. Susan said her
job was nothing special but she enjoyed it. Bill said there
were times when his music-playing did get to be special.
"Some of the places we play," he said, "you're taking your
life in your hands when you walk in there."

Fights, you mean, I said.

"No," he said. "Not fights. I mean, in one place, a VFW
lodge in south Alabama, we started playing and a damn
snake slithered across the dance floor, went between our
feet, and ended up under the juke box." He told it as a
Southerner tells a story: more interested in the humor of it
than in the possible consequences. A Northerner, I suspect, would have dwelled on the possibility of snakebite.
Perhaps because his environment made him more familiar
with snakes than most Northerners, Bill Bullard didn't
even mention whether the reptile were poisonous.

He and Susan were living together and not married,
and I asked them if the publication of that fact might
cause any consternation in Adalusia, which has a population of around 10,000. They said they didn't much care if
it did, but that they doubted it would. They were much

more interested in a couple of issues that seem to concern a large number of white Southerners. One of them could be called the OSHA question.

The federal Occupational Safety and Health Administration, a part of the Labor Department, had been widely regarded—not just by Southerners—as the very distillation of the nitwit bureaucratic mind, an agency that is supposed to protect workers' lives but that ends up doing things like requiring bridge builders to wear flotation vests while they work over dry gulches. (More recently, OSHA has promised to quit being so foolish. It remains, of course, to be seen.) Susan and Bill felt that OSHA's stupidity was making it harder for workers to work, and they resented that. Southerners, I was reminded once again, like work.

The other issue, very much in the public mind at that time with the Bakke case before the U.S. Supreme Court, was the matter of presumed reverse discrimination. It was the topic that had bothered Jack Breed in Mississippi. (Bakke, a white, was suing a school that had refused him admission while accepting members of minority groups who, he argued, were less qualified. In the end, the Supreme Court agreed with Bakke.)

"State jobs," said Susan, "used to be open for everybody who was qualified for them." (Well, I thought, *almost* everybody. Almost half of Alabama's population.) "But it's not that way anymore because they have to set a quota. You know, the Alabama Highway Patrol's only taking blacks now." Bill nodded an agreement. It was interesting, though, that neither did Susan and Bill complain violently nor did they whine about the problem. They spoke as if it were a phenomenon that they didn't particularly like, but one that they could live with.

Didn't it strike them as passably important, I said, that this alleged reverse discrimination was occurring in the state of George Wallace, who, despite his recent attempts to appear moderate, will surely be recorded by history as one of the nation's most prominent racists? And whose governmental decrees certainly didn't hold state jobs open for everybody qualified for them? Who inspired God knows how many people to violence against blacks? And whose highway patrol was one of the South's more formidable instruments of racism?

Susan and Bill grinned. Said Susan: "I don't think he ever believed anything about anything, race or anything else. He was just being a politician." She spoke of George Wallace in the past tense.

I meant to camp on Santa Rosa Island only one night, but I ended up staying three. The fourth morning I left, reluctantly, because I knew I should not spend all my time walking along a nearly deserted beach. But it was hard to leave, and five or six miles down the highway on Santa Rosa Island, in the direction of Fort Walton, where I would get the bridge back to the mainland, I stopped and strolled back over to the beach. There were no No signs, no official threats or warnings. It was easy to just pull off the road and park, although this was a national seashore, because it hadn't yet been properly discovered. It wasn't too crowded—yet. And that can be said for much of the South—yet.

I took off my shoes and walked in the warm jade surf for a few minutes, and then I turned and headed back toward the car. When I got there and started to dry off my feet for the return to socks, shoes, and civilization, I realized that there were large, sticky splotches of tar on the bottoms of both my feet. From an oil spill in the Gulf, obviously. It was everywhere in the beautiful water, and it was being deposited all along the beautiful beach that wasn't too crowded—yet.

13

Jay Carter

The handsome old brick building had had advertisements painted on its side since time immemorial, proclaiming the worthiness of patent medicines and soft
drinks now long forgotten. And now the ads, too, had
faded away, as had much of the town, which was Troy,
Alabama. But there was a set of fresh, homemade signs
stuck to the brick: "Flea-Market," said one. And "Jay's
Trading Post." And "Sale."

Jay Carter came to the door, as did a friendly-looking
woman of great age. Inside the building there were
clothes, gadgets, plates, toasters, trinkets, lamps, appli-
ances, the stuff of flea-markets everywhere. "This is my
mother," he said. "Miz Gertrude Carter. She's the best
friend I have, except the Lord." Mrs. Carter smiled
politely.

Jay Carter had been a cabinet maker until his firm had

laid him off. He collected unemployment, but it bothered him. "You'd have to go down to collect, and they made you wait half a day before you could get your money, and that just didn't appeal to me," he said. "I'm used to *working.*" He made the word sound good and solid. "I enjoy working. I certainly didn't like *not* working. So after a little while of unemployment, I said to myself, 'I got to get myself a job. I'll *make* myself a job.' That's when we opened this place."

Not too many people came as customers, he said, and those who did come didn't spend an awful lot of money. "It's been rough," he said, "but at least I've got a job. I live on hope." He said that last sentence calmly, matter-of-factly. It was, I thought, as I drove on down the road, a very dramatic thing to say, but Jay Carter had just sort of thrown it away, as if he thought of it as just a simple, everyday truth, not a dramatic declaration.

IV
Anticipation

14

A temporary detour from the highway to consider the arrival of a long-awaited event

When you travel through the South, you soon realize that despite the plastic and the interstates, the region is not in any immediate danger of being swallowed up by mainstream America. You see, all around you, the things that make the place uniquely Southern. Some of them are obvious and even stereotypical, the sorts of things that make such lasting impressions on tourist Northerners here on their first visits: things like politeness, and doing a day's work for a day's pay, and the mellowness of the accents, and the feelings for family and humor that still manage to survive.

There is another quality, though, one that I didn't expect to find but that I saw everywhere I went and heard no matter whom I was talking with. It is a feeling among Southerners of anticipation, of excitement about the South's future; a sense of being in on an important event that is in the process of happening. It's like looking into the faces of the crowd that always gathers when a movie company is doing on-location filming. I saw such a crowd once in Savannah, where Burt Reynolds was making one of his movies. A lot of the people were simply hoping for a look at the stars, but I sensed that more of them were excited about being witnesses to an *event*.

The event, here, is a much larger one, infinitely more exciting and promising and long-lasting: it is the economic fruition of the Southland. It has been long awaited in the South, by governor and sharecropper alike; long fought and frustrated by the money men of the North; long discussed by academicians and union organizers and editorial writers and regional sociologists. Now it is happening, and it seems that every resident of the South, no matter how removed from the immediate influence of this change, is participating in it—if not financially, at least emotionally.

So we have to stop the journey for a moment and examine some of the numbers that go into a definition of the modern South. Most of those that follow come from publications of the Southern Growth Policies Board; others are from the Census Bureau and various other federal government agencies.

The most obvious trend has to do with numbers of people. The South is growing in population and in wealth. The South (here it is a fifteen-state region that includes all the usual ones plus Maryland, Arkansas, and Oklahoma) contains a third of the nation's population and a quarter of its land. In 1970, the South and the West combined (what is popularly called the Sunbelt) had 8 million fewer people than the North (meaning the rest of the nation). By 1976 the South and the West had achieved a slight majority.

Another way of putting it, which doesn't take into account the West's growth, is that the nation's population increased by 11.3 million between 1970 and 1976; more than 6 million of that increase was in the fifteen-state South. Florida, the fastest-growing Southern state, had a twenty-four percent population increase in that time.

A major part of the population movement was attributed to migration into the region, which before had been characterized by what the Census people called "a heavy net migration loss." People of all sorts have been among the immigrants, but a large portion of them have been thirty-five or older, and many are retirees. As we have seen before, the long-standing trend of black migration out of the region, meanwhile, has reversed itself. Blacks who would have left haven't, and others have returned from the large, cruel cities of the North.

The chief reason for the population influx, almost everyone was agreeing in the late seventies, was the South's promise of employment opportunity. Industry, especially manufacturing, has been drawn to the South by lower operating costs (which include lower wages paid to workers, fewer illegal payoffs to crooks, police, and the like, and lower and fewer taxes paid to governments), an abundant supply of labor (including workers who are not pro-union), plentiful natural resources (especially water and energy), and an ordinarily mild climate. The South's economic growth has also been affected by federal programs (such as the Tennessee Valley Authority and various expensive navigation projects, subsidized shipbuilding, and a plethora of military installations), and by the tremendous growth in recent years of state government bureaucracy.

As the population and economy have swelled, personal income has risen faster in the South than in the nation at large. That doesn't mean Southerners get more money; their actual increase has been only about ninety percent of that of Americans in general. Florida, Arkansas, and Texas have experienced the greatest income growth; Georgia, North Carolina, Oklahoma, Kentucky, and Mississippi have had the least.

Black income, while still below that of whites, has been rising in the South. A decade ago, only two percent of the region's black families was making $15,000 or more a year. In 1974 the figure was thirteen percent. Attractive neighborhoods of housing for well-to-do blacks, and other visible signs of black entry into the middle class and beyond, once were peculiar to Atlanta and a few other places. Now they may be seen in most urban areas of the South.

Another source of Southern wealth has been energy production. Even during the worst seasons of unemployment in recent years there have been jobs available for skilled workers in the energy-producing states.

A sizeable portion of the South, though, black and white, has shared very little in the Sunbelt's boom, from energy or otherwise. Most of this group may be found in the rural areas. A Task Force on Southern Rural Development reported, in 1977, that "Rural development stands at the forefront of the unfinished business we consider of pervasive significance to the welfare of the United States. The extent of wasted human resources in the South raises serious moral and political issues."

In 1974, said the task force, the South was the home of about 10.8 million of the nation's 24 million poor people. Of the Southern poor, 6.1 million were white and 4.5 million were black. A little more than half of them lived in non-metropolitan areas. (In the rest of the country, only about twenty-nine percent lived outside various metropolises.) In terms of actual numbers, more white than black Southerners are poor. But the percentage of blacks in poverty is much higher than the percentage of whites in poverty.

The South has made massive advances in many other fields, just as it has in income, but again the tendency is to lag behind the rest of the nation. The per capita expenditure in the United States on public school education in 1976 was $314. No Southern state (unless you include Maryland, with its well-off Washington suburbs) spent more than that national average, and some spent quite a bit less: Mississippi spent $218, Arkansas $205, and North Carolina $282. (Expenditures do not necessarily reflect the true quality of education, however. New York State spent $408 per child but its biggest component, New York City, has a school system that is shot through with waste and wrongdoing and routinely graduates illiterates. Janitors in New York schools make more than many college presidents, and some have their relatives on the payroll besides.)

Health care is improving in the South. Infant death rates in 1974 were virtually the same in Georgia as they were in New York, and in Mississippi as they were in Nevada. In *all* parts of the country the black baby has a little more than half the chance of a white baby of living to the age of one year. It has been estimated that the South would require 14,758 additional physicians to bring its doctor-patient ratio up to the national level. (Some may question here, as with educational expenditures, whether more necessarily means better.)

The situation is improving, or so the statistics indicate. No longer is the Southerner automatically consigned to what the rest of the nation terms a second-rate existence. No longer does the sensible Southerner with the price of the ticket leave the South as soon as possible. Indeed, people from the rest of the country are descending on the South in droves. Interestingly enough, many of the newcomers are not making their homes in the traditional precincts of the immigrant—the big cities. They are heading for the non-metropolitan areas of the South, and that trend could have a profound effect on the region in years to come.

Twenty or so years ago, a classical scene was repeated every Saturday in every Southern city: The farmers came to town.

In Raleigh, my hometown, they would park their pickups around the downtown squares. Some would sell fresh vegetables and eggs to the city people. Almost all of them would visit Montgomery Wards or Hudson-Belk or Briggs Hardware; and some stopped by the Alcoholic Beverage Control store as well.

Most of that is gone now, in Raleigh and elsewhere, although farmers' markets have been reborn on the fringes of some cities because urban people have rediscovered fresh produce. For a great variety of reasons—including the construction of high-speed highways, the rise of agribusiness and the decline of the two-mule farm, the explosive growth of suburbia, the belief that free parking is a constitutional right, and the virtual disappearance of the traditional downtown department store—the structure of the Southern population and economy has changed.

The South has become a society where neither downtown nor the farm is as important as it once was. Life has followed the more affluent citizens and is centered now in the *metropolitan areas*, rather than their central cities, and that means much of it is built around the suburban shopping centers, which, in turn, can mean anything from a Muzak-soaked mall designed by an architect to a sleazy ten-mile-long strip of retail stores, fast-food joints, and transmission shops.

The Southern farmer and city-dweller cross paths on Saturday afternoons now in the parking lots of these shopping centers, and it is becoming increasingly difficult to tell them apart. They wear the same denim and permanent press from the K-Mart; they drive the same sort of sporty pickup trucks with the same sprouts of silver antennas on top; their educational levels are not all that different; the things they're shopping for are the same; and very often they pay for them with the same kind of plastic cards, on which interest is collected by the same banks.

One result of all this is an often-pleasant blending of the styles of living of the urban and rural South. The countryside is never far away, either geographically or emotionally, from most Southern city-dwellers. Nor is the resident of the countryside excluded from the pleasures and stimulations of the city.

The region abounds in symbols of this new amalgam. A standard roadside feature of the rural South used to be the obligatory auto or truck tire that hung by a rope from the tall oak or willow and that provided at least as much childhood joy as the most sophisticated set of playground swings. Now you see kids playing in tires that hang in suburban back yards, and when you look closely you find that the tires are steel-belted radials with raised white lettering.

In 1974, a thoughtful document called "The Future of the South" reported the development of this trend toward rural and urban amalgamation. The report was dispatched by the Commission on the Future of the South, made up mostly of educators and businessmen, to the Southern Growth Policies Board, whose chairman at that time was Governor Jimmy Carter of Georgia. The report said, in part:

"Despite large areas of the South that remain rural, the majority of Southerners now live in a society in which the traditional distinctions between rural and urban lifestyles have lost their meaning. City and countryside shade into each other, creating a new and more diffuse pattern of human settlement.

"Most Southerners—whether they live in an urban, suburban, or rural setting—shop in the same chain stores, work at the same kinds of jobs, commute to many of the same services, share the same radio, newspaper, and television services. Only in the mountain counties of the Appalachian heartland and some areas of the Coast Plains are large numbers of Southerners still living outside these patterns."

Demographers have discovered that much of the South's phenomenal population growth is occurring not in the large central cities but in outlying areas—smaller cities and towns, suburbia, and exurbia. Such growth is found throughout the region, according to a report by E. Evan Brunson and Thomas D. Bever, but especially in the mountainous parts of Georgia, Tennessee, North Carolina, and Virginia; the coal fields of West Virginia and Kentucky; parts of Alabama and Tennessee influenced (and polluted) by the Tennessee Valley Authority; the Ozarks and Ouachita Mountains of Arkansas and Oklahoma; north central Mississippi; the Cumberland Plateau of southern Kentucky and northeastern Tennessee; central and southern Florida; the hill country of central Texas; and parts of the coastal Carolinas.

Several central cities, in the meantime, are losing population to the suburbs and exurbs around them. Exurban growth is occurring particularly around Nashville, Atlanta, Knoxville, Chattanooga, Oklahoma City, Little Rock, San Antonio, Austin, Orlando, Washington, D.C., Birmingham, Houston, and practically all of Florida. Simultaneously, though, some cities—notably Atlanta and Houston—are becoming national and international centers.

All the indications were, by the late seventies, that this pattern of growth would continue, barring, perhaps, only a crushing energy crisis that would make walking to work not only good exercise but also mandatory. Industry—not just the low-wage sort that in recent years has typified much of the Southern economy, but, increasingly, firms that pay decent wages—will also continue to seek out the non-metropolitan areas. There they can find supplies of workers who are "willing," cheap land, abundant water, and relatively low energy costs.

So what we are witnessing is a phenomenon that may be called the "suburbanization" of Southern work: a movement away from the traditional forms of agriculture, but not really toward the sort of manufacturing that characterizes the steel towns and milling centers of the industrialized Midwest and North, either.

The South's fastest-growing industries between 1970 and 1975 were services, followed by a category that included finance, insurance, and real estate; then followed by state and local government, and retail trade. ("Services" comprise a variety of businesses, from motel management to photo studios, auto repair shops and advertising agencies and a lot in-between.) The categories of slower growth included agriculture and manufacturing (although more Southern workers—a quarter of the total—are employed in manufacturing than in any other single field).

That 1974 report on the future of the South raised a point that since has become a significant one: "The South may have leaped the 'manufacturing era' experienced by earlier urbanizing areas," said the document, "and entered an era . . . in which information, technical skills and services will dominate the society. As the South advances, it will have to prepare for a high services economy and all that will mean in terms of the production, distribution, and consumption of knowledge."

As you look around the South, now, you have to conclude that much of the region has already entered that era. And as you listen to the political and economic leaders of the rest of the nation, particularly the Northeast, you will hear mounting expressions of resentment against the South's good fortune. The resentment is already so great that those who study and guide the South's economic growth have started to downplay the by-now familiar stories of Southern and Sunbelt success, and to remind themselves and their fellow Southerners that the region is still short of economic perfection.

The South does have a lot of problems. Not surprisingly, many grow directly out of the region's great successes:

A shocking portion of the South's population is still dirt poor, despite the fact that income levels are rising. And there is a distinct danger that the South's poor will be forgotten. That risk grows as the South experiences further development. As the network of interstates and look-alike airports and chain-motel–and–restaurant–shopping-center living becomes the rule in the South as elsewhere, it becomes easier to bypass, literally and figuratively, the pockets of deep poverty in the South Carolina Lowcountry, the upper coastal plains, the hollows of Kentucky, the Mississippi Delta, the black and poor-white sections of Atlanta and Houston and Memphis.

An abundance of energy has had a lot to do with the South's economic growth. But the future is uncertain. The South produces seventy-two percent of the nation's energy, but much of it is exported out of the region. The South uses a lot of fuel and power, too: individuals in the region consume about twelve percent more energy than the national average, and Southern industry uses twenty-five percent more.

One of the nation's last relatively unspoiled resources, the Southern seacoast, is in jeopardy. It is conceivable that this treasure, once seemingly as endless as water or air, can become a ghetto of oil refineries, condominiums, and mobile home parks.

There is a danger, too, of an escalation of what *Business Week* somewhat exaggeratedly referred to as "The Second War Between the States: A Bitter Struggle for Jobs, Capital, and People." In that connection, by the late seventies there was a belief, widespread in the North and other sections of the country, that the South and the Sunbelt were getting an unfairly large share of economic help, including grants and contracts from the federal government. Sixteen "Snowbelt" states organized themselves into a "Northeast-Midwest Economic Advancement Coalition" to seek more federal funds.

It is standard political rhetoric in the North—a rhetoric repeated by the politicians so often that it has become a myth, recited by the very lowest levels, which is to say the New York cab driver—that Northerners' tax dollars disappear at the time of collection into a sort of underground railway, the next stop on which is the sunny Southland. The South, meantime (so the story goes), pays virtually nothing for its own support and adds insult to injury by "exporting its problem to the North." This is a Northern white liberal/racist code phrase meaning that many black people from the South have migrated to the North. It is generally assumed by many better-off Northerners that blacks come to the North specifically to wallow in near-luxury on welfare.

Some challenges have been raised to the Northern arguments. Walt Whitman Rostow, the economist who served the Kennedy and Johnson administrations and who then went on to teach at the University of Texas, explained in a speech to a Massachusetts audience that the Northern argument, in crude and not entirely correct form, was that "the rise of the Sunbelt was a product of disproportionate outlays of the federal government financed by Northern taxes" and that "now is the time for the South to contribute disproportionately to the rehabilitation of the North."

The Birmingham News, in an editorial on the subject, put it this way: "What the Northeast wants . . . is a second Reconstruction." The newspaper reminded its readers that the first one was not aimed at rebuilding the South for the South's benefit, but rather for the North's.

And E. Blaine Liner, the executive director of the Southern Growth Policies Board, said in a speech that "Northerners who are anxious to look elsewhere for explanations of increasing economic impotence at home too often seek refuge in a simplistic reliance on regional prejudice. In short, they blame the South for the bleakness of the North."

The controversy may provide some satisfaction for Southerners who delight in hearing, after all these years, the allegedly superior North whining about the South's successes. But some Southern thinkers have counseled almost a turn-the-other-cheek approach to the problem. The semi-official line seemed to be: Downplay the South's advances so as not to antagonize the North; extend a great deal of sympathy to the Northern sufferers; make no visible efforts to raid the industries of the North; make the point frequently that *every* region of the country needs economic development, and that a national effort should be mounted to provide it; and, simultaneously with all these friendly and polite gestures, don't let those poor-mouthing Yankees take a single federal dollar or a single job away from the South.

The line also calls for disseminating studies and reports

which counter the Northern allegations of disproportionate federal aid. One such study, done in 1976 by two government economists, concluded that the claims of a big shift in jobs and industries to the South had been exaggerated and could not be supported by hard facts. Still, a large number of Northern politicians and even average citizens continued to maintain that the South was progressing at the expense of the North.

There was a certain irony in all this, inasmuch as the North progressed very definitely at the expense of the South during most of the nation's history. Some Southerners, then, see the situation as one in which the South is merely trying to do something that the North has done. And this brings up the dilemma that many see as the most formidable in the South today: the danger that, in becoming economically successful, the region will turn out to be just like the North—and that it might very well lose its soul in the process. Some call it the "trade-off issue": How can the South continue its economic growth and retain the qualities that make it, for many of its citizens, a superior place to live? How can one policy be gained without trading off the other?

In a sense, this is directly connected to the region's identity. Without the qualities that make it "the South," the South ceases to exist. Or—and to some this is the ultimate horror—it becomes just another North, a place where everyone hurries angrily with no place to go, where human preys on human, where common decency is unusual, and, most dramatically, where the environment and quality of life have largely fallen victim to simple greed.

Until fairly recently it has been the policy of the Southern states to encourage economic growth without worrying too much about the sort of growth that was being encouraged. North Carolina, under former Governor Luther Hodges, sought "clean" businesses many years before industrial pollution became a national issue, but there are many other places that traditionally have wanted industrial growth so badly that they didn't worry about the air that the workers' families breathed or the water they drank. And so we have the foul-smelling papermill towns of the Georgia coast, Piedmont textile factories that treat workers like chattel, the noxious furnaces of Birmingham, the automobile pollution of an Atlanta that grew too fast, even the poisonous air put out by an agency of the government itself, the Tennessee Valley Authority.

This policy of growth at any cost has changed dramatically in much of the South in more recent years. Politicians, non-elected leaders, members of the academic community, and ordinary citizens are discussing the new issue constantly now. Former Florida Governor Reubin Askew said not long ago that the question had become "how the South can sustain stable economic growth without abusing our human and natural resources and our cultural traditions." Walt Rostow, speaking of the larger geographical entity of which the South is a major part, said: "The challenge to the Sunbelt is, of course, to complete its transition to industrial modernization; to develop its resources in energy and agriculture in both its own interest and that of the nation; to deal with its social problems, under conditions of rapid population increase; and to do all these things while avoiding to the degree possible the environmental degradation which marked the urbanization of the North."

Very few Southerners, in the meantime, seem to be advocating a "no-growth" policy, in which the Southern environment would receive the ultimate protection from industrial intrusion. In other parts of the nation, advocates of "no-growth" are frequently vocal, and of right ought to be, because they are surrounded by so many examples of harmful growth. Every expansion plan that is advocated by New York's infamous power monopoly, Consolidated Edison, is opposed by large numbers of citizens, who know from painful experience just how incompetent, arrogant, and dangerous the utility can be.

In the South, there seems to still be some faith that economic advancement can be properly managed—although there are increasing examples of the reverse. Duke Power Company, for instance, is well on its way to matching Consolidated Edison. But most Southerners seem to share the hope of editor and writer Sylvan Meyer that "We can grow without sacrificing the very amenities of good water and air, mountains, seashore, Spanish moss and piney woods that form the basic assets of the region."

Doing all that, of course, is the neatest trick of them all. Conferences, convocations, retreats, and seminars abound throughout the region as thinkers and leaders (and occasionally some leaders who are also thinkers) try to find a way. But the heartening fact is that Southerners are trying at all; for that means they think the battle can still be won.

"It's a double-edged sword," said Blaine Liner of the Southern Growth Policies Board. "It's nice to become like the rest of the nation economically. But we have to be careful about that other edge—the negative side. The technology we have now gives us a big advantage, plus the examples that we can see of the other parts of the country that aren't pleased with their urbanization."

A lot of people agree with that assessment—that it is to the South's advantage that its economic maturity had been retarded through the decades following what some still call "the war," because that means it can now use new technology to avoid the environmental mistakes of the North. It's as if the South is leaping from mule-drawn plows to sophisticated cultivating machines without having to spend any time in between. As examples of that sort of technological leapfrogging, Liner offers some of the region's well-designed housing developments and its environmentally healthy industrial complexes.

One of his colleagues, John De Grove, agrees. De Grove is the director of the Florida Atlantic/Florida International Joint Center for Environmental and Urban Problems at Fort Lauderdale. He said in an interview that he felt the South was indebted to the "horrible example" syndrome, in which leaders and followers agree that "We've still got time in the South to avoid the mistakes of the North."

"I think the South profits very strongly from one thing," he said: "The emergence of the environmental consciousness of the Sixties. It caused a fundamental change in the attitude of the people in this country about the cost of growth."

Growth started in the South *after* the formation of this consciousness, he said. And so the growth has been better managed, and it reflects more respect for the environment, than the earlier growth that characterized the more affluent areas of the country and that resulted in the plundering of so many natural resources.

And the consciousness is strong among Southerners. "For a politician in the South to run overtly on a platform of being against the environment would be political suicide now," said De Grove. "The notion that there's an environmental limit beyond which you can't go is engraved in the voters' minds."

Such a feeling exists in some degree all over the country, of course. But it's especially noticeable, I have found in this journey, in the South. In New York, "the environment" is often a one-issue thing, related to an individual's own comfort and livelihood: homeowners in the flight path of the foolish Concorde airliner protest it but those outside don't; shad fishers fight the pollution of the Hudson River, but they do so in relative isolation. The politicians of the North barely pay lip service to the notion of protecting the environment; their much more fundamental allegiance is to the power brokers—the realtors, bankers, and big labor unions—whose entire survival is closely aligned with the continued exploitation of the environment, with little or no concern for what happens afterwards.

In the South, the environment is part of the entire notion of life. A Southerner can be in favor of more jobs, for development of the coastal area, even for experimental alternatives to the traditional methods of producing energy, and can still be considered an environmentalist. The Southern environment is part of every Southerner's vocabulary, and that fact may figure importantly in the salvation of the region.

15

The capital of the New South

"If you're not into suburban living," said the friend, "you might not like Houston." I'm not, and I don't. I didn't stay in Houston any longer than I had to.

Houston is tasteless, garish, ugly, and mean. Its police force has been shown to be undisciplined and dangerous, and I suspect those traits, rather than being problems of just the Houston Police Department, reflect the whole place's hatred for those who have not made it in this world—for the people who, because of their color or language, are not among those who possess the power to make deals over lunch in some architecturally profound downtown office skyscraper.

Equally profound writers from New York have flown down and looked around and declared Houston to be America's city of the future. Human greed being what it is, it's quite likely they are correct, in which case I soon shall have to conduct a gigantic yard sale and start living on a sailboat. Houston's one redeeming factor is that much of its economy is built on the unchecked consumption of petroleum by human beings and their machines— so it is possible, and even likely, that some of those of us now living will be able to witness Houston's great collapse when that petroleum runs out.

It was on a Sunday morning that I decided to run out too. Downtown Houston's air was awful, in both quality and quantity (I say quantity for it could easily be captured and held momentarily in the hand, like wood smoke or the dust devils that languish under beds and sofas), and I realized that staying around was just foolishness. So I announced to my friend my intention of heading for Galveston via public transportation. It was about sixty miles from my hotel, in downtown Houston, to Galveston.

"You mean renting a car," said my friend.

"No, I mean public transportation."

"There *is* no public transportation here," he said. "Everybody has a car." We placed a small bet, although his conviction in the matter had pretty well convinced me that I would lose. I won, however. A funky old bus makes the run, stopping everywhere in between. Its coaches are to modern interstate Greyhounds and Trailwayses as the old DC4 is to a 747, but they do go to Galveston and back. And so I presented myself at the Houston bus terminal at 8:30 on a Sunday morning, bound for Galveston.

The central portions of many cities—nearly all, I'm sad to report—exist now, during evening hours and on weekends and major holidays, for the near-exclusive use of the people of a certain under-culture: the downtown people. These are the people who do not buy their denims at the K-Mart, and who do not hang steel-belted radials in their suburban back yards, because they never get to suburbia.

They don't own cars. They don't own homes. They are the people of the downtowns. Many are white men, and almost all have ceased to be of any "importance" to the remainder of society. They are never written about in the newspapers, even when they are born or when they die—and not even when the occasional one of their number takes a knife in his hand and ends the suffering of a woman he has lived with for decades. Nor do they figure into the thinking of educators, sanitarians, lawyers, internists, speech therapists, orthodontists, psychologists, psychiatrists, podiatrists, social workers, television market consultants, the U.S. Census, Master Charge, *The* New *New York Times,* Clay Felker, Dr. Joyce Brothers, Barbara Walters, Johnny Carson, Channel Seven's Action News Team, the civil rights movement, the women's rights movement, the gay rights movement, the Italians Are Number One Movement, the Native American rights movement, any other movements, sociologists once they have secured tenure, almost all newspaper reporters, portrait painters, Social Security, the Law Enforcement Assistance Administration, the Secretary of Health, Education, and Welfare, or even the hookers who share the streets with them.

And their friends? I'm not sure they have very many. There are some places where the downtowners are not ignored, though; where their presence does not cause immediate revulsion; where they may even be welcomed: the downtown liquor stores tolerate them very nicely, because some of them are good customers, buying horrible wine at exorbitant prices. Western Union accepts them. Western Union makes its money off businesses and satellites and other such deductible junk, but in order to keep its monopoly it must maintain a few telegraph offices for the ordinary public—and most of these are downtown. They serve the downtown people as banks; places where people who do not have checkbooks can send and receive money from, to, who knows? And a few hotels know these people, hotels you will not find listed in your *Mobil Travel Guide*. And a few smelly downtown taverns, places where drinking is not a social occasion. And, most of all, the bus stations.

The bus driver looked like a Ku Kluxxer until he took his sunglasses off, and then his eyes looked soft and kind, and I realized he was probably a grandfather. He stood by the door of the old coach, taking tickets and making sure we were getting on the right bus and answering questions. Only four of us got on that morning. Besides me, there was a man of about thirty who wore white pants and a white shirt with a white tee-shirt under it, and two older men who had seen much of the world. One was smoking as he got on, and there were bulges in the coat pockets of both the older men.

"You can smoke in the back but you can't drink here," said the driver, who knew from experience what the bulges were. We all got on: I sat at the front so I could see the landscape; the two men went to the back row, and the younger man in white took a seat a couple of rows from them. The driver checked his watch, honked his horn at the dispatcher, cranked the door closed, and maneuvered the old bus out of the station. It took special knowledge to shift gears without scraping, and the windshield had a large crack in it.

We passed a Whataburger, and a Jack in the Box, and a Cash for Your Car, massage parlors, Seven-Elevens, Motel Adult Movies in Rooms, a U-Totem, Bob Abernathy's Chevrolet, a Tune-R-Up, signs that said "Drive Friendly," Resurrection Cemetery, The Scripture Shoppe, Pizza Hut, Steaks, Chops, Shakes, the Starlight Club, the Star*lite* Club, the Canine Clippe Joint. It was as if all the lower-middle-class people of Houston and environs had decided to get equal time for the corporate tastelessness of downtown.

"I been heading offshore for three months but I ain't got there yet," one of the older men was telling the man in white. They were talking about offshore oil-drilling rigs. "I ain't worked my real trade for six years," he continued. "I was up in Colorado for a long time. But then I got divorced and I haven't done much of anything since then. What you, a cook?"

"Yeah, a cook," said the man in white clothes. "That ain't my *trade* job. My *trade* job's welding. But I ain't done it for a long time. I was out there on a rig and was freezing my balls off and this old boy says to me, 'You know what, it's *cold* out here.' And I thought about that and sure enough, it *was* cold. And I walked off that place and haven't been back since. Started cooking on the rigs. It's inside work, and good pay, and a hell of a lot different from being outside on a rig. I get three-seventy a week and ain't cold, warm showers and T-bones every Friday and Saturday."

You could tell that the other men were somewhat envious. One asked if the cook was heading offshore when he got to Galveston, and he said he was. He talked some more about what a good deal he had. He said he'd been in Houston for his days off, but was happy to be getting back out into the Gulf.

"I lost my teeth in Dallas, I tell you that," said one of the older men. He had been drinking out of his paper bag. "I'm forty-four and I got a long way to go, I tell you that," he added. He looked much older. He was toothless and his eyes looked rheumy. His skin was like boot leather that had been through a hard winter without being taken care of. The man in the cook's whites agreed that he certainly looked like he had a long way to go. The cook was acting a trifle condescending in his dealings with the older men, especially the toothless one, who did most of the talking.

"I tell you how I lost 'em. I'z riding a freight one day and I sneezed and them goddamn teeth went sailing out the door at sixty miles an hour, no way on God's earth I was gonna get them mothers back again." He laughed and the cook laughed with him. "And I'll never ride a freight train again."

The toothless man and his friend got off in Alvin, about half-way to Galveston, and headed for a roadhouse. The bus, the man in cook's whites, and I continued on to Galveston. The cook sang softly a song about Houston, the sort of phony-sounding song that is about Texas but that was written and made famous by somebody who lives in California. When we got to Galveston, the cook told the bus driver he was going out into the Gulf that afternoon and would see him in three or four weeks.

That evening, after walking around Galveston for several hours, I waited at the station for the bus back to Houston. Three or four other people were waiting, too, and one of them was the young man in cook's whites. There were patches of dirt on his pants and shirt now, and in his hip pocket was a pint bottle of something in a wrinkled paper bag. As he got on the bus for Houston he looked a little tight, and also very discouraged, as if his job had not been waiting for him in Galveston.

Atlanta is much more like it, much more of what the capital of the new South should be.

I lived there during the civil rights confrontations of the sixties. That was when the city got its head start on the other contenders. While the white leaders of places like Birmingham and Jackson were destroying their communities with violence and repression, Atlanta was trying to live up to its reputation as "a city too busy to hate." The slogan started out as little more than an advertising claim, conferred on the city by its white business leaders, few of whom wanted integration but all of whom desired a social climate conducive to economic growth. Turning a buck. It helped immeasurably that Atlanta had a black middle class that was strong politically, intellectually and, relative to other places, economically.

Later, as some peaceful desegregation began, Atlanta started calling itself a "national city." And more recently the promoters have been referring to it as "the world's next great city."

The greatness is easily identifiable, if your definition includes physical objects. Atlanta's skyline is massive and impressive, the result of a building boom some years ago that almost, but not quite, went sour in the recession. (*The New York Times,* which is not immune to the disease of Northern business chauvinism, runs frequent front-page stories on Atlanta's economic troubles, which are nowhere near as serious as those of New York. The stories themselves are fairly honest, but the headlines are usually of the catastrophic variety, on the order of "Once Proud City on Chattahoochee faces Doom, Eventual Dismemberment.")

The population of Atlanta's metropolitan region, which stood in 1977 at something like 1.8 million, is spread over a huge area. The freeways are jammed night and day, in no relationship to the usual rush hours, like those of Los Angeles and New York.

There are other kinds of greatness, too: a broadening of the town's political environment is one of them. The old boys in the downtown power structure, who had their own man in City Hall for decades, more recently had to suffer through a term by a mayor whom they didn't much like (partly because he was Jewish and somehow never got invited to join their clubs), and now some of them have actually assisted in the election, and then the re-election, of another mayor who didn't come from their stable—

Maynard Jackson, one of the very few black mayors in America.

And in the years since the building boom started, something else has happened to Atlanta: it has become a true, full-fledged city, a place where you can get anything, do anything, live comfortably but close to the action; a city worth visiting not because you have relatives or business there, but just for its own sake. There are ethnic restaurants, great varieties of entertainment, drama, sports, intellectual stimulation, the arts. An extremely important event is the city's declared intention to get away from the usual self-destructive dependence on the automobile by constructing a rapid transit system.

Which is not to say that Atlanta is all sweetness and light. Jackson appointed a black to head the police and fire departments who behaved not too differently from some of his white contemporaries, and who was finally let go. There is a good deal of white flight to the vapid suburban areas. *Atlanta* magazine, a once-gutsy publication that was the model for slick city magazines, and that since has become a parody of itself, is now edited and published in Sandy Springs, a well-to-do white suburb. But some interesting things have happened.

The downtown whites, who in the mid-seventies had issued a statement complaining that Jackson's attitude was "perceived [by them] as anti-white," and that people [they meant whites] were getting worried over the "racial mix on streets [meaning too many blacks]," more recently have found themselves quite friendly toward the mayor. They liked the way he has managed the city's finances, they liked the way he's compromised on a few issues, and they especially liked the way he broke a municipal workers' strike.

"It's clear to me," said Dan Sweat, the president of Central Atlanta Progress, Inc., not long ago, "that Maynard learned that if you're going to run this city, you've got to run it with the support of the business community, among other groups."

Largely because of the mayor, Atlanta seems now to be headed into yet another era. Maybe the national city that was too busy to hate and that's on its way to world status can become, along the way, a city that respects and keeps its neighborhoods.

While Jackson was running for his first term, in 1973, a big issue was the proposed construction of an interstate highway through the northeastern part of the city. Homes, many of them belonging to upper-middle-income whites, would be destroyed. Jackson pledged then to resist the project, and out of that successful effort has come an increased awareness, in City Hall and in the neighborhoods themselves, of the power of neighborhood organization.

The new mayor established Neighborhood Planning Units, through which residents have obtained a measure of leverage on what the city does to their environments, from street lights to police protection. And there has been an additional, fascinating development: the downtown whites started trying to help preserve and nourish the neighborhoods, too.

Back in 1973 many businessmen had viewed neighborhood organization as an enemy. Those who resisted the interstate highway, they felt, were blocking Atlanta's progress. But since then, they've learned that slogans and even hotels with revolving barrooms on top are not enough. Dan Sweat's office is still loaded, as it has been for years, with fancy maps and balsa-wood models of all the construction completed and envisioned in downtown Atlanta, but he is speaking now of neighborhoods as the big item on the agenda.

Sweat's organization has created something called the Atlanta Mortgage Consortium, which in 1977 was acting

as the funnel for $62.5 million for mortgages and rehabili-
tation of in-town neighborhoods via loans that were, it
claimed, "competitive with loans being granted in the
suburbs." Central Atlanta Progress also put together a
consortium to undertake the multi-use development of a
seventy-eight-acre tract of urban renewal land, left over
from two decades ago, near the heart of downtown Atlanta. The project, known as Bedford-Pine, is supposed to
result in three thousand living units, an office complex,
shopping center, and an unusually large (twenty percent)
amount of open space. Other programs aimed at stabiliz-
ing Atlanta's neighborhoods were in the works.

"We've come to the conclusion," said Sweat, "that the
economic health of downtown depends on more than the
shiny new buildings downtown. We're not going to have
an international city unless we have good neighborhoods."

16

Tidewater city

If you look at it on a good road map, you won't see just one splotch of color marking a single city. There will be a profusion of colors, arranged in irrationally-shaped geographical patterns abutting the light blue of Chesapeake Bay and the James River and, connecting those two bodies of water, Hampton Roads.

Norfolk, the best-known of the geographical areas, will appear inordinately small, almost pushed into the water by a giant blob of color named Virginia Beach. Surely the beach couldn't extend that far back from the ocean, but the legend on the map says it does. And Chesapeake and Suffolk, which are largely made up of swampland but which are also identified as cities. Portsmouth, another sailing town that was settled early, huddles with Norfolk against the Roads. On the other side of the straits lies Newport News, home of the naval shipyard, and Hampton, which was settled in 1610 and thus became the first permanent English community on the North American continent (Jamestown, not far upstream, was abandoned).

So that area which might once have gone under the name "Norfolk" is no longer just that. You have to call the place "Tidewater" now—a rapidly-growing metropolitan region composed of several diverse communities. It's quite likely that the Tidewater area has got a lot to do with what many Southern cities are going to be like in years to come. Whatever *that* is, no one seems quite sure. One man who moved to Tidewater several years ago from Ohio commented, after he had been there a while, that it was indeed a strange conglomeration. "Part of it's established city, like Norfolk," he said, "and part of it's the future, whatever that's going to be."

What makes the Tidewater area different from many other places, both on the map and in real life, is the way in which the suburban communities have developed. Norfolk and Portsmouth, the older cities, were, for a long time, surrounded by water and by agricultural land— land that, if anybody thought much about its political allegiance, was considered the property of a *county*. Hampton and Newport News and the cities on the mainland side of Hampton Roads developed into a separate metropolitan area of their own—largely because of the water barrier between them and the other cities. There was a combination bridge-tunnel over and under the Roads to Norfolk, but its operators exacted a toll.

A few miles southeast of Norfolk was Virginia Beach, but it was exactly what its name implies: an ocean-front development, largely for the weekend and summertime amusement and recreation of the people who lived farther inland.

In the early sixties the situation changed, according to

Dr. Wolfgang Pindur, a political scientist who directs the graduate program of the Institute of Urban Studies and Public Administration at Norfolk's Old Dominion University. "What happened," he said, "was that you had the counties trying to take over the cities of this area. So you had Virginia Beach, which at that time was really just the resort strip, merging with its county." A result was the instant creation of a city-county close to 300 square miles in area, or almost ten times as large as Norfolk. Virginia Beach has since become one of the largest cities in the country in terms of geography, although its population (172,106 in the 1970 Census) makes it considerably less than a giant. That population, however, has the money to buy and maintain homes in the best suburban tradition. "Projections are," said Pindur, "that Virginia Beach will have a relatively old population, but a rich one. It's the place where the military officer who retires goes and probably gets a second job."

Chesapeake, largely agricultural except for the territory that forms part of the Great Dismal Swamp, did the same thing with its county, and now Chesapeake is even larger than Virginia Beach. "So," explained Pindur, "you have this kind of anomaly of a city, where the major industry is agriculture and, in the case of Virginia Beach, in addition to agriculture, it's tourism."

Virginia Beach and Chesapeake have relatively little in common with Norfolk and Portsmouth; Suffolk, an even larger agricultural community with an even smaller population, has even less. What the various components of the entire region *do* share is found in the area's name—the Tidewater. It implies an association with, if not a dependence on, the mixture of salt and fresh waters that flows past Hampton Roads. That association is not just a nostalgic one. The area is burgeoning with military installations, most of them connected with the sea. Partly because the region is attractive to military employees once they retire, partly because it is one of the northernmost cities of the Sunbelt and therefore lures retired persons from other regions, Tidewater is a good place to live in once the pension starts. The climate is warm but not Deep-South hot; Virginia has a relatively progressive state government; and the larger cities of the Northeast are not all that far away. And there is a great deal of recreation available in any direction. It is quite possible to live the good life in Tidewater Virginia, if you have the inclination and the money.

In addition to a chance at the good life, Tidewater offers an example of a condition that may soon become commonplace among the middle-sized cities of the South: a metropolitan area (or, strictly speaking, two of them, for they remain separate in the eyes of the census despite the recent dropping of the bridge-tunnel tolls between Hampton and Norfolk) in which the older, somewhat more rundown city center finds itself in competition with its surrounding suburbs. It is a situation not unlike that which has prevailed for many years in the North. One very important difference, though, is that the suburbs' strangulation of the northern cities has been going on so long that the cities are barely alive, while there is still time for rational growth to occur in the South—growth in which no one has to suffer.

I asked Wolfgang Pindur, whose urban institute pays special attention to the area surrounding Hampton Roads, if that were the sort of growth that was occurring in Tidewater.

"Absolutely not," he said. "That's been one of our personal frustrations here. A colleague and I met with Virginia Beach leaders from all segments of the community at a two-day goal-setting meeting. We developed goals for the city, particularly in the area of growth management. We got all these goals agreed upon. And they are doing absolutely nothing to implement them. The frustration is, none of these cities has had a growth plan. None of them is willing to recognize the costs of sprawl that's not channelled or managed, or whatever word you want to use. It's a serious problem in Virginia Beach. Their community development funds go almost ninety-five percent to sewers. So what they're really doing is extending the city and beginning to encroach on the agricultural land. . . . It's growth by accident."

Growth by accident might not have such decisive and divisive effects if there were more freedom of choice within the Tidewater area in matters of housing. As it stands now, in Tidewater, as in a hundred metropolitan areas around the nation, the choices are somewhat narrowed. If you are a "suburban type," you live in Virginia Beach or Chesapeake, or possibly in Suffolk. Norfolk and Portsmouth draw those who are the adventurous "urban types"—the young-couples-on-the-way-up who have the money, the commitment, the enthusiasm, the optimism, the time, and the energy to buy old houses in dilapidated condition and turn them into elegant homes. There are several renaissance neighborhoods in Norfolk. And the cities also draw—"keep" is the better word—those who might well want to live elsewhere, but who are restrained from doing so by the color of their skins or the condition of their pocketbooks or, as it so often happens, by both.

And so suburbia grows; and it grows, as Wolfgang Pindur puts it, without much guidance. I asked if perhaps, in the absence of direction from elected and appointed officials, the standard power structures could be expected to provide leadership. We talked about Virginia Beach, since that serves as the leading example of the suburban side of Tidewater.

"The power structure in Virginia Beach," he said, "is basically builders, hotel owners, and construction people. And the farmers. There aren't many environmentalists around, and almost no people who believe in land management. Virginia Beach is a city of two hundred forty-some thousand now, and it has a professional planning staff of, I think, five. And the city up until recently was adding up to a thousand new residents per month."

You sound pessimistic, I said. What do you see happening in the future?

"I suspect what's going to happen is, you're going to see in Virginia Beach, first, and then in Chesapeake later, and in Suffolk at some point in the future, the urban sprawl example again."

Like Long Island? I shuddered as I asked the question, thinking, as the words came out, of the lovely great island that had been ruined by horrid housing developments, racially and ethnically restrictive communities, the most irrational sort of shoreline "development," and an awful political machine.

"Yes, very much in that character," said Pindur. "I'm very frustrated by the fact that Virginia Beach is not willing to look at the cost of growth: only willing right now to look at the benefits of it; where growing is considered the thing we all want to do."

I asked him what he thought should be done?

"I think what we need," he said, "is a very strong regional planning organization. Right now, we have a very weak, cooperative one. And such an organization would need to develop a regional land-use plan, and regional plans for even such things as the dispersal of low-income housing."

From time to time, he said, there was talk of setting up a select committee to make recommendations on region-wide issues that might be too hot for the usual politicians to handle. But the proposed blue-ribbon group would represent only the most conspicuous members of the Tidewater community, Norfolk and Virginia Beach. The area-wide approach would still be lacking.

"I think it's bound to fall short of success because it's a

regional-wide problem," said Pindur. "Until we have a regional agency with clout to make and enforce policy, we're just going to kind of stumble along. For the future of this area, as I see it, we're going to stumble along as it is: with a little bit of cooperation here and there, and a lot of people scratching their heads and saying, 'We've got to do something' about this or that. Until there's a real crisis."

17

The heart and soul of the city

I realized, as my journey progressed through the summer, that I wasn't spending much time in the cities of the South. In discovering the pleasures of staying off the interstates, I was reducing the amount of time I spent in the places that are connected by those interstates—places that have goodly numbers of their own pleasures, and that should not be neglected.

But in the process of staying on the secondary roads, I discovered the beauty and dignity and greater simplicity and the basic decency of a lot of places I had never thought much about before—the smaller cities, the towns, the country crossroads, the farmhouses along the highways. There is a good reason for my affection for these places: it is in such places that many of the good and interesting qualities of the region have been least diluted;

where the individualism and good humor of the place most easily show through.

This accounts in great measure for my repeated and intemperate attacks on the enfranchised roadside South, too—the proliferation of copying-machine images of everything from portion-controlled roast beef sandwiches to deodorized cow manure is a distinct threat to the future of the Southland as I know and want to remember it.

But I cannot properly blame the cities of the South for fast-food franchises and fifty-acre K-Mart parking lots. Those are really the products of suburbia, which is perhaps the greatest single enemy American society has at the moment, barring a return to politics of Richard Nixon and Spiro Agnew. There's a lot of good going on in the urban centers of the South, and much of it has to do with rediscovering and rebuilding parts of the cities that once flourished, and that got temporarily left behind in the post–World War II jump to suburbia.

The older neighborhoods of a thousand Southern cities, from Little Rock to Birmingham, are being revived, and in some of them (such as, for instance, Atlanta) there are verbal—and sometimes material—commitments from bankers, image-builders, realtors, and the like—the same sort of people who, by their previous exercise and abuse of power and capital, destroyed downtown housing to build parking lots and expressways and simultaneously built suburbia to provide a means for filling those expressways and parking lots. There are even a few documented cases of city bureaucracies actually trying to make it easier for idealistic, energetic homeowners to use their own funds and sweat to turn deteriorating housing into taxpaying, useful property. (If you sense a bit of irony here, you sense correctly. I happen to think that bureaucracy is society's second greatest enemy.)

Both Charleston and Savannah enjoy worldwide reputations for the way their city governments have helped the cause of historic preservation, although Charleston appears to have gone off the deep end. (How else can you describe a town that passes a law requiring horses to wear diapers, and that boasts loudly of its great restaurants when it has only one? Alexander Woollcott once said that at the end of Charleston's garden season the tourists leave, providing Charlestonians with "no one to despise but themselves.") Far more often, though, the people who presume to run the cities work against the salvation of those very cities. Consider the conversation I had a year or so ago with R. V. Asbury, Jr., the director of Historic Wilmington Foundation, Inc.

Wilmington is to North Carolina as Charleston and Savannah are to South Carolina and Georgia, although it is several years younger. It lies near the mouth of the Cape Fear River and has a relatively large historic district. But the restoration fever has not been as strong in Wilmington as it has been in some other places, and on the day I saw him, Asbury seemed to be particularly despondent. It still was much easier, he said, to destroy an old house in Wilmington than to preserve one.

You own an 1840 house in Wilmington, he said, and for some reason decide to tear it down—the reason often being that you can't afford the money and energy and heartbreak involved in fixing it up. Or maybe you just have no feeling for old houses, or maybe a fast-food chain has offered you some money for the property. You apply for a demolition permit from the Historic District Commission. The application may very well be denied, he said, "but the catch is, the denial is only good for ninety days. So after a ninety-day waiting period, if some agency like our foundation hasn't bought the house, or if you have not been persuaded by embarrassment or coercion of some type by the citizens or your neighbors, or maybe if you don't want to sell it to us—you tear it down. And that's the way it is, all over America.

"We've lost a lot of buildings even after the ninety-day period. In twenty years we've lost two hundred buildings that were one hundred years old. An then it goes to two hundred one, and two hundred two, and two hundred three—when does it end? There has to be some level reached by the citizenry where they say, 'We have now reached an appreciation plateau, or a cultural plateau,' and where they pass laws to protect these old houses. And if you don't have these restrictions and statutes and ordinances, in my opinion, all the dumb-asses in the world and the lunatic children who grow up to become mayors and city councilmen—they'll have *everything* torn down."

As he was saying all this, Asbury was gesticulating wildly, as if he were on a stage delivering a lecture to troops about to go into battle. He said, when I asked him, that he felt his line of work, the preservation movement, "has all the scholars it needs. It needs people who have a little bit of showbiz, a little hustling, a little understanding of real estate and planning and just a tad of being an expert in history. You need a showman, a con artist who can get up and hustle and dazzle the public. That's what it takes to raise money. People might not like those kinds of phrases, but that's what the hell it's all about." That and educating the public and the bureaucracy. Asbury said one of the big problems of historic preservation in Wilmington, as opposed to places such as Savannah and Charleston, was convincing the various city housing inspectors that old houses are special.

"It's a very desperate thing when you're fighting time," he said. "We're talking about a building that's been here since 1840, 1850, or 1870. But because some building inspector's reading a damned manual, and he says the building needs to be painted, the fate of that building is going to be determined by a person like that. Many of them have been demolished because of this.

"The inspector says he's just doing his job. Technically,

he is. But you say to him, 'They're building factories and they're building hospitals; why don't you go out there and inspect *them?* This house has been here since 1840. It ain't going to fall down tomorrow. It will look a little worse, I'll grant you. Maybe some shingles will blow off of it. It needs paint. But if it's lived through all these wars we've had and all these hurricanes we've had, and the Depression, it can stand another six months or another year.'

"And the inspector says, 'Well, they're an eyesore. And I can't treat this area any more specially than I can treat another area.' And then I say, 'Well, you *should*, because this is the heart and soul of the city.' "

When the houses have been saved and a new generation of people has moved into them, their special ability to serve as heart and soul becomes even more apparent. There is never a time in the life of an older city neighborhood when the people who did the restoring can take an extended break from their work. There is always something to be done to the house, and there is always some threat from the outside world, like a rumored expressway that would obliterate the place, or some halfwit bureaucrat's plan to chop down all the trees. But there are moments when old-house people can exchange their paint-stained blue jeans for their nicer casual clothes and gather for drinks and conversation and not a little self-congratulation.

There was one of those gatherings not long ago at the home of Bill and Jane Crump, who live in Richmond's Fan district. (It is called that because its streets form a fan pattern.) The Fan, the best-known of several renaissance neighborhoods in Richmond, is close to downtown, and its houses, which date from the beginning of this century, are pleasant and comfortable. It is not unusual for residents of the Fan to speak derisively of their friends and business acquaintances who live in suburbia. In Richmond the West End is the stereotypical suburban settlement. I asked one of the women at the gathering how she would describe the West End.

"I would describe it as Sunnybrook Farm," she said, without hesitating. "Split-levels and tri-levels, and the occupants have minds to match." Someone else mentioned that property taxes in the West End were half what they were in the Fan, and that the city did relatively little to encourage the old-house movement. But the compensations were great, they all agreed. "What I like so very much," said Diane Moore, "is that where we live there's a conglomeration of ages, from seventies to newborn. One of the things I find so lovely is that, while the culture has obliterated the extended family, our children are still exposed to elderly people. And in a very casual way. These people are on the street, and visiting with us, and being friends, and sharing nice experiences with us. And so the children learn a great deal just by their own street experiences, besides learning elementary survival."

"There's another thing that's very positive about this neighborhood," said someone else. "You can hardly walk out your door without tripping over another child and another adult. But nobody *bothers* you. In the suburbs, everybody's always coming around saying 'Let's go bowling tonight,' or 'Let's go drink a beer.' They're always hanging over the fence. But here, people don't bug you. They respect your privacy. If you go into your house, that means you want to be left alone. If you're out front, that means you want to talk to somebody."

"Not only are our children being exposed to other people," said Diane Moore, "but our children also get to know the pharmacist around the corner, and the man in the little grocery store, and the policeman who patrols the area, and the mailman. These are people who our children are exposed to every day, and they know each other by their names. It's sort of like the environment you had in the 1900s in New York, where everybody had their neighborhood market and drugstore and beer hall and whatever. It sure beats suburbia."

18

W. W. and Clara

Luverne is a small town in southern Alabama, a quiet, peaceful-looking place. I passed through it at a respectful speed and on the way out I saw a simple country store. At first glance it seemed like a hundred others you'll see if you travel on the old roads and keep yourself from becoming preoccupied with getting somewhere in a hurry. But this one was different.

"CLOSED FOR GOOD," it said, in what looked like white spray paint, on one of the big windows. Under that was the name, "CLARA."

W. W. Mathews came out of the house next door. He had seen me stop in front of the store. He didn't act at all suspicious; just curious as to why I was there. So often in the South the assumption in a situation such as this is that the stranger is on peaceful business. Elsewhere, it is more likely to be that he is up to no good. And there are places in the South, too, where this suspicion is beginning to take over.

I explained why I had stopped, and W. W. Mathews asked if I wanted a cup of coffee or something.

"I closed the store because my wife died," he explained. She was Clara. "I built it in thirty-nine. Built it mostly for her. I was working at other jobs, and the store was something for her."

There was a tone in his voice that said he didn't mean he had built the store as just a plaything for his wife. It had been a place where Clara could use her talents, her brains. W. W. Mathews turned and looked at the silent building. There was a screened box out front, and in it three chickens pecked away at the floor.

"I was working at other jobs," he said, again. "Sold Pepsi-Cola on a route truck for twenty-one years, and then ten years selling Standard Oil. I'm on Social Security now." He was tall and thin and bony, but he looked alert and strong.

"This was Clara's store. Not really my place. She enjoyed working in it. Ran the whole thing. I closed it once before, when she was sick, but when she came to her final sickness I decided to close it for good." He looked lonely.

19
Cosmopolitanism

It was only a few years ago that I walked into a pizzeria in Raleigh and ordered a pie to go. The proprietor was an Italian-American who spoke with a Southern accent, and he seemed much more courteous than most of the purveyors of take-out food back home in the North.

Did I want cheese on my pizza? Of course, I replied, a little surprised, since in those parts of the world where there's a pizza stand on every corner it is assumed that the fundamental element of any successful pie is generous sprinkling of mozzarella.

Fine, said the proprietor, and he opened his refrigerator, removed a brick of Kraft Velveeta Process Cheese Spread, minced a half-ounce or so of it, and sprinkled it on top of the pie.

I swore off eating pizza in the South then, and I charged

off the entire incident not to the pizza-maker's ignorance (he probably *liked* mozzarella on *his* food) but to a certain lack of cosmopolitanism on the part of the people—the Southerners—who formed his clientele.

There has been traditionally in the South a certain distaste for, and sometimes an active hatred of, people and things and tastes and smells and styles of living that were out of the ordinary. Southerners of my acquaintance, including some of my own relatives, were quick to put someone down because of the clothes he or she wore, or their hair styles, or sometimes even the books they read. You could get in serious trouble in, say, Monroe, Louisiana, for walking around wearing Earth Shoes. A "foreign" license plate, in some places, meant you were an agent of evil— perhaps an advance scout for some modern-day General Sherman. A rioter in Mississippi once accused me of having fallen under Northern spells because I was from Atlanta, which to him, in those anguished, confused days, was as foreign as Boston or Spokane.

All that has changed or is well into the process of changing. I still don't dare eat pizza in the South, but I've found that in many other areas the region has become as cosmopolitan as the great majority of the rest of the country. Some for instances:

The pleasures of the palate are available in the South now as never before. Joel Fleishman, a North Carolinian who has worked with politicians and educators (some of whom were both) at Yale and now at Duke, commented that "Within five minutes of my house [which Fleishman wisely maintains a dozen or so miles away from Duke, in Chapel Hill], and within ten minutes if I walk, I can get more different kinds of cheese, more varieties of tea, than I could get in the entire city of New Haven. I can get ten or fifteen kinds of fresh coffee beans, which I have roasted to order. And two hundred kinds of spices, and as many different kinds of wine, imported and domestic. And that situation's not limited to Chapel Hill."

Multi-purpose civic arenas, which can serve as music halls, exhibition centers, skating rinks, athletic coliseums, and lecture halls, all with some quick manipulation of the seats and stages, may be found in dozens of Southern cities. Touring companies, from the major symphony orchestras to the current rock phenomena and off-Broadway shows, play now in communities that have always had the potential of enthusiastic audiences but that before were never on the circuit.

There now is (or at least was, until the chain went out of business) an Earth Shoe store in Monroe, Louisiana. And there are places called Unisex Hair Salons in Mountain City, Tennessee, and in most other towns of the South.

In a Safeway store in Warrenton, Virginia, you can buy Chinese bean curd and refrigerated tortillas. A baker in Richmond turns out 1,200 loaves of Middle Eastern *pita* bread a day. There are several authentic Indian restaurants in Southern cities. You can choose your own live lobster from a tank at a Winn-Dixie supermarket in Asheville, North Carolina. (But in the same store I sought to buy one onion. All the produce had been mounted, like animals fresh from the taxidermist's, on green cardboard slabs encased in tightly-shrunk plastic. There were no single onions. I explained to the produce manager that I wanted only one onion. He sighed and took a slab of half a dozen onions into the back room. He returned, four or five minutes later, with one onion, carefully wrapped in plastic in the middle of its own big chunk of green cardboard. His waste of materials and energy probably surpassed the cost of growing, harvesting, and shipping the onion. At no point, until I had left the store, was I allowed to actually touch this thing that had been pulled away from the warm earth and that soon would be radiating its essences into my stew.)

When you ask for a glass of the house wine in a Southern restaurant now, you may get not the traditional blank stare but something quite good—although the selection is still likely to be limited to the brands advertised on national television.

The reasons for this apparent increase in cosmopolitanism, and what appears to be a corresponding decrease in insularity, are numerous. For one thing, the Southern population, like the nation's, has become increasingly mobile; people bring different, sometimes exotic, tastes with them when they move to a new town. The decline of race as an obsessive factor in the white South has meant that people and ideas that once seemed strange—a man with a beard, a woman with very long hair, a "natural" food store, sandals, marijuana—are no longer viewed as threats to the social order, or what passes for a social order. As the troubles of the non-South have increased and have been written about and discussed, the South has finally learned it isn't inferior at all; it can relax its guard against foreign ideas, can afford to sample from the tastes and sensations available in other cultures. And the World War II baby boom, along with the South's acknowledgment that it needed to improve its educational opportunities, caused a proliferation of community colleges that have exposed hundreds of thousands of Southerners to the tastes and interests of people unlike themselves.

Twenty years ago, when I was finishing up college in Chapel Hill, William Friday had been appointed the head of the Consolidated University of North Carolina. That meant three basically white institutions, in Chapel Hill, Raleigh, and Greensboro. Now Friday's empire, like those of his colleagues in other states, stretches from one end of the state to the other, and covers something like 100,000 students on sixteen campuses.

One result of this expansion has been depersonalization (especially when you consider that the University of North Carolina opened in 1775 with one student; the president was also the professor). Today, the university will not even consider a student's application unless the student supplies his or her Social Security number. But another result of enlargement has been the refinement of a sense of service, by the colleges and universities, to their state and region that is simply not found in the North. I asked Friday about the old argument that there were no Harvards in the South.

Comparing a Southern university with Harvard is a waste of time, he replied, because you're not comparing similar things. Chapel Hill is part of its community, its state, and its region in a way that Harvard can never be. "I would assume," said Friday, with just a small smile, "that there are people at Harvard who would really like to see their university be as effective as this university in terms of servicing the region and the nation.

"But the important point is that in this region over the last quarter-century there have been *many* universities that were, let us say, good, established institutions that have now become really *great* institutions. The process has matured. The South has institutions in it that can hold their own with any other region of the country." And, in the bargain, that can and do bring the excitements and stimulations and depressions of the world outside to their communities, freeing the South, for better or for worse, from some of its parochialism.

Another reason for the South's cosmopolitanism has undoubtedly been the stuff that comes over the broadcast spectrum. Commercial television has been blamed, and rightly so, for crudely leveling the tastes of all Americans. The radio station I grew up with, WPTF in Raleigh, is still stuck in the bland past; it plays music so bad that it goes *beyond* renditions by Tony Orlando and Dawn into *imitations* of renditions by Tony Orlando and Dawn; at one point not long ago the record that got much of its airtime involved someone singing like a chicken. And throughout the South there are FM stations playing wall-to-wall pap that is slightly worse than that normally encountered in an elevator on the way to one's dentist's office.

But increasing numbers of Southerners are exposed to high-quality offerings on public television channels and on the National Public Radio network. Texas, Tennessee, South Carolina, and Virginia make particularly good use of non-commercial radio.

And there are books. The South once was viewed by much of the literary establishment as a vast Dogpatch, populated by illiterate rubes whose joy at not buying books was surpassed only by the pleasure they got out of burning them at school-board bonfires.

Now books are selling very well in the South. One of the reasons is that imaginative young people have taken books out of the dimly-lit corners of department stores, where they once languished next to piles of Bibles and cookbooks, and put them into well-laid-out bookstores where they belong. Wallace Kuralt is one of those young people.

When Wallace's older brother and I were at Chapel Hill twenty years ago, there was one store—the Intimate Bookshop—where you could feel the innate *warmth* of books; where you could gaze and browse and fantasize and go home with something really valuable in your hands. Now Wallace owns the Intimate, or rather the Intimates—two in Chapel Hill, two in Charlotte, and one in Fayetteville, North Carolina, and he owns the Savile Bookshop in the Georgetown section of Washington, D.C.

—and he is a bookselling czar. He has serious doubts that Southerners aren't interested in books.

"It's not just that we're in a college town," he said. "It's all over the place. All it takes is an entrepreneur who cares and who has the money and has the pride in what he's doing—and bookselling has a lot of that pride—and it'll work." He has set up a non-profit organization to help people get into the business.

"People used to think Southerners didn't read books," he said. "When we were opening up our first shop in Charlotte, everybody said we were doomed; that Charlotte was a 'bad book town.'

"Well, it *was* a bad book*shop* town, not necessarily a town where people weren't interested in books. What it needed was somebody who was willing to go out on a limb and stock something more than just inspirational books and light fiction. We [he meant his co-owner and wife, Brenda, and Charlotte partners Barbara and Eric Svenson] went out on that limb and people came into the store and took books off the shelves like they were loaves of bread. The market was there, just as the market's there in a lot of places throughout the South. People just haven't had a place to buy books before, or to buy and do a lot of the things they've wanted to do. And now all that's changing."

V
The harvest

20

Enfranchisement

The summer was ending now. The solstice was imminent, and the more practical mark for the end of the season, Labor Day, the date that meant the children must go back to school, had passed. And yet the heat went on—it seemed on some days to be stronger than anything July or August had offered—and the growth continued, though more slowly now. The foliage was a deep, dull green, less lively or luxuriant than it had been; more elderly, enfeebled, moving now toward death. The drought had broken in most places, but the rain had come too late and many of the crops had been declared ruined. Away from the cultivated fields, deep in the woods where nature made less oppressive demands on the growing things, the summer dryness was hardly noticeable, except for ferns close to the ground. In many places they were simply burned yellow. But they, or their seed, would be back next year.

The harvests—the ones that go on in the reality of the cornfields and orchards, and the ones that take place in the mind, at the end of a summer of growth—were only now beginning, and there were still several weeks before the great old state fairs would sweep through the Southland, when the sweet warmth of the days would be counterbalanced by the invigorating chill of the lengthening nights, and people would start thinking seriously about winter again.

I rolled along a country road, doing maybe forty-five, headed generally in the direction of the coast again, smelling the air and gorging my eyes on the delicious sights. The road was precisely wide enough for the traffic that used it; the road and the farms and houses alongside were in perfect proportion, perfect scale with one another. Then, suddenly, the scene changed.

The oil-company signs appeared first, an American and an Exxon, on tall masts that must have been sixty or seventy feet high. The two-lane road suddenly widened to four. Then I saw the Holiday Inn and the Sunoco and Gulf signs, and the road went to five lanes and started climbing a small artificial hill. The hummock had been built over Interstate 95. I slowed down in the middle of the overpass and looked at the traffic below. Cold, heartless, bored, desperate, looking straight ahead, fighting off the sleep that comes from monotony. The traffic made an endless, roaring sound. Northerners headed for Florida, Southerners headed back to college, truckers headed everywhere.

The country road descended the other side of the hummock, passed the Exxon and American, went to four lanes again, and then, as the sound disappeared and the little road finished its brief convulsion over meeting the superhighway, it went back to its accustomed two lanes and continued, slowly and properly and with great dignity, on its way to the sea. It took me past a sad little combination grocery store–drive-in–eating place, and the owner was sitting outside on a lawn chair. A sign said "If you can't stop, wave," and I waved at him. He returned the greeting.

So much of the life of the South is built along the mental equivalent of secondary roads. Because the region was retarded, by the Civil War and then by its continuing problems with race and all along by the hatred and exploitation of the North, the equivalents of the primary roads—the interstates, the urban renewal, the shopping centers, the suburbs, the economic development in general—were painfully slow in coming. But now the money is there. The energy and humanpower are there, and the South is building, expanding, growing, attracting money and people. And the pressures to give up the secondary roads are tremendous. It would be nice if the new could be achieved without abandoning the old.

I went into a Seven-Eleven, which had a sign advertising the fact that it was now open not from seven until eleven but twenty-four hours a day. I looked at the magazine rack for a copy of *Esquire,* in which a piece of mine was running. It looked as if there were no *Esquire.* There were plenty of movie fan magazines, and knitting and crocheting magazines, and publications designed to help you find out what is on television and how to buy a used car. There were no copies of *Esquire,* or *Harper's,* or *The Atlantic,* or the best one of them all, *The New Yorker.*

The clerk asked me if she could help. I explained that I was looking for the current issue of *Esquire.*

"What kind of a magazine is it?" she asked.

"Well," I said, "it's kind of a magazine for men." It was difficult to describe *Esquire* then—this was before it came under new ownership and got turned into an imitation of *New York* magazine. *Esquire* then, although it was having its troubles, could still best be described as a magazine of considerable editorial excellence and no particular formula.

"Well," said the clerk, "the men's magazines are in that special section over there." She directed me to a separate rack that was built in such a way that everything but the flags—the nameplates, or logotypes—of the magazines, was hidden from view. *Oui, Playboy, Penthouse, Hustler, Chic,* and more I never heard of. This was what magazines for men were in the Seven-Eleven.

I yearned for the old newsstands of a hundred downtowns, often hard by the main post office. They were places where you could get newspapers from halfway around the world, and magazines of every description, and even little literary journals from colleges tucked away in the hills. They would get the magazines and put them on the racks even if only half a dozen customers seemed interested.

I slept in a motel and started out early the next morning, hoping to make a few miles before stopping for breakfast. After a while hunger overcame me and I foolishly stopped at an outpost of a chain joint. I asked them for one of their egg concoctions. The smiling counter lady had it all there in an instant in its little hinged styrofoam box that would soon be a clutter upon the landscape: an egg cooked some time before and then maintained at some theoretically perfect (but in practice awful) temperature that had been selected by a committee or a computer or both; a copy of an English muffin presumably laced with preservatives; other ingredients that might have included cheese; and, for some reason, a safety razor, which the chain was giving away as a promotion that month. Everything but a napkin, which I didn't really need because the food product was congealed and there was no danger of its running down my arm toward my elbow when I bit into it, the way it does with a properly-prepared fried-egg sandwich.

Twenty minutes later I was a dozen miles down the road, my neck tensing at the prospect of an imminent intersection with an interstate. I was thinking those random, non-earth-shaking thoughts that you think when you're driving, and somehow my mind lit on the subject of breakfast. For some reason I could not recall whether I had eaten breakfast. The memory lapse went on for three or four minutes. My stomach told me I had eaten, but my brain, or soul, or whatever it is that is involved in these matters, really couldn't remember having been satisfied. I might as well have chewed up a handful of raw soybeans.

On another morning: I went through a city, out and away from it on a freeway, running against the mainstream the way I like to, the traffic helicopters overhead, the unhappy people facing me. After seven or eight miles the road became two lanes, but alongside it the earthmovers were running back and forth, laying the bed for an extension of the freeway. I stopped at Anne's. Both the motel and the restaurant bore her name. It looked like a place where I might get a good Thermos of coffee. The buildings were whitewashed and an old-fashioned sign outside the motel read "Steam Heat Air Con." A big old Freuhauf sixteen-wheeler was parked out front, carrying no load, its motor running at an erratic Diesel idle.

Inside, a young woman in a white waitress's uniform sat at a table with the driver of the truck. She was lean and pretty and a Southern-looking woman, the skin around her eyes wrinkled more than it should have been because she had seen a bit more life than she should have. She smoked a cigarette and fiddled with a cup of coffee. The man wore a grey uniform, smartly-pressed like a Greyhound bus driver, with a cap, and a shoulder patch from his trucking line, and Western-type boots. He seemed ill-at-ease when I walked in, as if maybe he was not supposed to be there. He relaxed a bit when I asked the young woman for a Thermos of coffee.

The restaurant was simple and unpretentious and extremely clean. Sanitation Grade A; Lunch Special $1.39 Hamburger Steak-Turnip Greens-Rice-Dessert-Coffee. I walked over to the juke box. Half the entries were hand-lettered and most of them were country and western. One just said "Loretta and Conway." The patrons knew their artists on a first-name basis.

The young woman put the plug into the Thermos and wiped the top off with a cloth and handed it to me and smiled for a moment. "You have a safe trip, you hear?" she said. I told her I hoped she had a good day, and I nodded at the truck driver, and I left.

Someday Anne's will be on that freeway, or maybe it will be obliterated by it. The chances are very great that it will be replaced by something more attuned to freeway living: a Howard Johnson's, or a Horne's, or a Stuckey's, all of them, in my estimation, good places to stay far away from.

The young woman might get a job in the new place. But would she have a chance to sit at a table with her trucker? Would she tell people to have a safe trip? What would her attitude toward people be? Would it be different, would it make her different, working for a corporation that couldn't care less whether you had a safe trip or not?

As I drove away I mourned again the passing of a part of the Southland, mourned it in advance. But I knew that others had mourned it, and some had loudly proclaimed the South "as we know it" to be dead and buried, gone, just another myth laid to rest; and I knew that the death had not yet occurred. I knew, too, the truth of the words I had been hearing all through that season of Southern warmth. *It's not too late.*

21

The Southern seacoast

All summer the people along the mid-South coast had been waiting for the hurricane. A big one, they said, was long overdue: a storm that brings the usual destruction of high winds, but that also pushes enormous amounts of water into the sounds, causing extensive flooding. And they talked about how strange the weather had been all year. Similarly strange weather, they said, had preceded the big storms of other years.

A whole new generation of homes, condominiums, and motels has risen along the coast since the truly big storms last hit. And, on the North Carolina coast especially, acres of mobile homes have sprouted along the seashore. The younger owners of these places, one suspects, have not seen the destruction that hurricanes can cause. People have built second homes along North Carolina's populated banks in precisely the places where inlets were violently cut during storms a decade or so ago. High-rise condos and motels have been built practically on the high tide line, and you wonder how much it'll take for a storm to push them over.

Jay Sheppard had finished the job of strapping his small trailer down to the ground. Now he sat in front of it, reading a paperback book. He had been born a few hundred yards away, in a farm house on a road that runs from Washington, North Carolina, toward Pamlico Sound. (They call it "Little Washington.") When he was old enough, he left Washington and went into the civil service, working with the Navy in locations all over the world. One of those places was the Mariana Islands of the Pacific, a place some consider to be quite lovely. Jay Sheppard thinks the South Pacific is fine, but that eastern North Carolina is finer.

When he retired, he came back, got a tiny trailer just big enough for himself, and parked it under a tall pecan tree on the edge of his brother's property. He has, he said, everything he needs now. "The trailer's fine for somebody who's living by himself, and I've got my moped to go get groceries on." His little motorized bicycle was parked nearby. Most of all, he had the great pecan tree. Its shade covered the whole yard. Beyond its circumference, it was a hot, sticky day, but in the shade it was cool and airy, a perfect place to sit, read a paperback and watch life go by.

"I had to strap the trailer down," said Sheppard. He referred to the metal strips that went around the trailer and into the ground. "It's the law now. They say that'll keep it from getting blown away when the hurricane comes. I doubt very seriously that it'll help at all, but it's the law."

Andy Denmark lived up the street from me in Raleigh. His father was a fine and locally famous portrait photographer who had a studio in a corner of Hudson-Belk's department store on Fayetteville Street, and who could make the plainest baby look lovable, or at least make him smile. Sometimes, before color processes became so commonplace, Andy's father would hand-tint his photographs for you.

The fact that Andy is three years younger than I is of no importance now, but back then when we were young it meant he was just one of the neighborhood's "littler kids," scarcely worthy of mention or memory except when he got in the way of our roller-bat games. So it was a little surprising that he and I remembered each other when our paths crossed again during this journey. Andy was no longer a little person; he had grown tall and robust and had gotten married to Mary and become the father of Melissa, and he and Mary own a sailboat marina in Oriental, North Carolina.

Oriental has changed, too. When I went there almost thirty years ago, it was the home of a few shrimp boats, and when the boats came in everybody went down to the docks and helped unload and shell the catch. Shrimps were forty cents a pound then, off the boat; shelled, then de-veined, they went for sixty cents. Of course, we never appreciated what a great bargain we were getting.

Now Oriental is a fine-looking community on the north bank of the Neuse River, not far from where the river opens into the vast and wonderful Pamlico Sound. Hundreds of boats are harbored at Oriental, and lots of them are sailboats with high-sounding names (like "Escargot") painted on their transoms above the names of land-locked cities (like Raleigh and Greensboro and High Point) that once hardly even claimed a canoe. Oriental's future, one might say, looks good. And Andy, Mary, and Melissa Denmark are part of that future. But it didn't come easily.

Andy, who was thirty-nine this summer, finished school as an industrial manager. His work consisted of finding everyday, civilian uses for the scientific and technical developments that were coming out of the nation's aerospace program. The work was interesting, but Andy soon grew restless with its theoretical nature. "I needed to get my hands on something that was real," he said.

He already was coping with the reality of wind and weather on weekends in a little sailboat he had bought. Andy soon changed jobs, this time to one that required him to be on the road from Sunday nights until late Fridays, and "every single soul I dealt with during the week had a problem for me to solve. It was a bit depressing." When he came home on Fridays, he and Mary would hitch up the sailboat and go off for a weekend of sailing.

Then a builder of racing boats in Virginia's Tidewater area offered Andy a partnership. Andy loved it until the recession hit and people stopped buying sailboats. Soon after he left that job, they discovered that Mary was pregnant. Andy took the only job he could find, which involved teaching industrial arts in the Berlin, Maryland, high school. They continued sailing whenever they could, and sometimes things got a bit tight. They remember one occasion when their refrigerator was empty except for one frozen fish they had caught previously. It was a spot, which is certainly edible, but hardly one of your more gourmet specialties. Andy and Mary debated about whether to eat or use it for bait: they took the risk, and Andy cut it up for bait. He caught a large and delicious sea bass for dinner.

And then, in 1970, a routine medical examination showed that Andy had cancer.

It was cancer of the thyroid, which has a relatively favorable survival rate. "If you've got to have cancer," Andy remembers the doctor telling him when he was breaking the news, "thyroid cancer is the one to have." But still, cancer is cancer. Its detection causes rearrangements of one's life. "Cancer," said Andy, "is a great eye-opener. Up until then I had thought I was immortal—not that I'd live forever, but that I had just never thought much about *not* living. It was pretty traumatic." The gland was successfully removed, in two operations, and once Andy finished the long and depressing adjustment to a synthetic hormone that regulates his metabolic levels, he had no difficulties.

But he and Mary did change their way of living. "We decided to do what we'd always talked about," said Andy, "which was to go someplace near the water, someplace that was really enjoyable, and all we asked was that we be able to make a living. We came up with a very detailed plan." The plan called for finding work to keep the Denmarks alive while they scoured the Southern seacoast for a place to live and a means for making a living. They moved to Raleigh for two years while Andy worked at a regular job; all their spare time was devoted to studying maps and exploring the coast, from Chesapeake Bay to South Carolina. "And we kept coming back to Oriental," said Andy.

When they moved to Oriental, in 1972, there was only a handful of sailboats. But the Denmarks knew that the area was perfect for sailing; it is protected, but it has easy access to the huge sound and to the Intracoastal Waterway and to the nooks and crannies of eastern North Carolina's rivers. So they built a marina on Whittaker Creek, over a marsh so full of beer cans and bedsprings that it took them four months to clean the place up. It took much longer to deal with the reams of paper that state and federal bureaucrats, who previously had shown little interest in Whittaker Creek, suddenly started throwing at the Denmarks.

Slowly, carefully, Andy and Mary complied with every request, filed every plan, rewrote every proposal, waited while the rubber-stamp artists composed their frequently unintelligible replies. Eventually they were able to open an attractive, twenty-five-ship marina, which they named "Sailcraft."

Andy feels (and the layout of the place bears him out) that he is every bit as much an environmentalist as any of the bureaucrats. He will fight to keep his side of Pamlico Sound, or Oriental, or Whittaker Creek, from becoming like so much of the rest of the coast. "The key to the whole thing," he feels, "is proper zoning laws."

"In a way," added Mary, "the position we're taking is a contradiction of our business."

"That's right," said Andy. "Our business is geared to the growth of the area. But we don't want too much growth. Growth has got to happen; everybody knows that. The question is, will it be within proper boundaries?"

At the moment, the Denmarks think Oriental is quite close to perfection. "I have the distinct feeling," said Andy as the big orange sun went down behind a forest of masts and shrouds, "that civilization is here, and not in Raleigh, or New York, or Chicago, or Philadelphia, or Detroit."

But might the time not come when they'll have to go searching for another Oriental?

"Maybe so," said Andy. "I don't know. If we do go looking, it'll be by boat. The boat will be our home." He had his big tanned arm around Mary, out there on the dock, and he squeezed her softly, and looked down at her and asked, "Do you remember the feeling we had of being trapped, with no control over our lives?"

"I sure do," said Mary. "It seems like a long time ago."

Of all the physical qualities of the Southland, the one that least resembles the remainder of the United States is its seacoast. From Ocean City, Maryland, north to beyond Portland, Maine, the East coast has been pretty thoroughly profaned: an uninviting line of condominiums and high-rise motels that blocks the view to the sea; a place of oily water and oilier hamburgers. The West coast is in better shape, its rocky palisades falling peacefully to sunset beaches that face toward another world, but development has taken much of it away from the people.

The Southern coast is different: a land of incalculable biological energy, of incomparable beauty, of romance and love and nature's violence; of mysterious lush islands and serpentine salt marshes. It draws us back time after time, some of us only in the summer, some of us whenever we can conjure up an excuse to return. You may have noticed that I have not been shy about spending much of my journey there.

The Southern coast starts with Virginia's eighteen barrier islands, moves down along the Outer Banks and North Carolina's mighty sounds; past the grand strand of South Carolina and then that state's Lowcountry islands and Georgia's Golden Isles, where people still speak a language delightfully different from the rest of us. Then around the Florida peninsula, a coastline that's as long as the nation is wide; past the tacky Miami Beach hotels and along the white-sand beaches of the Gulf side, and then past the industry and playgrounds of Alabama and Mississippi; the rich delta of the Mississippi River in Louisiana, and then down the long Texas crescent, first clogged with industry and smelling of the sort of quick money that cares little about the environment, and finally ending in a broad, beautiful beach on South Padre Island near the Mexican border.

The shoreline is 19,227 miles long, if you count the length of the bays and estuaries as well as those of the ocean and gulf. This equals fifty-three percent of the nation's shoreline. Most of the Southern coast—sixty-two percent—is privately owned. Thirteen percent is owned by the federal government, twelve percent by states and local governments, and the ownership of the remaining thirteen percent is uncertain. A surprisingly large portion of it—seventy-two percent—was still undeveloped in 1971, when the Corps of Engineers surveyed it. Thirteen percent was in non-recreational development, nine percent was devoted to private recreational use, and six percent was set aside for public recreation.

The Southern coast, with or without all the statistics, is a priceless resource, more valuable to us than all the oil refineries, all the interstate highways, all the jetports in the nation. And it is in danger of being lost. The danger comes from the fact that we have assumed for so long that we could take whatever we wanted from the coastal area; that the resource was inexhaustible. Consider some of the things we have done:

We have churned away at the dunes in order to erect beach cottages, second homes, and mobile home parks, and then we have watched in amazement as the beach we have just weakened—more valuable to us and the banks now that we have built things on it—erodes. Instead of learning the obvious lesson from this, we have spent our tax money pumping more sand onto the beach. We call this idiotic process "nourishment."

We have mined the coast's minerals and fossil fuels; filled in marshes that serve as nurseries for all sorts of seafood; put groins, jetties, and breakwaters out into the ocean; constructed industries that pump sweet water from the underground aquifer and, after using it, returned it loaded with poisons. We have further destroyed the dunes with recreational vehicles and, in the case of some of the uninhabited stretches of the North Carolina banks, when our vehicles have broken down we have left them where they stopped, corroding steel carcasses on the beach.

We eat with great gusto the creatures that come out of the wetlands and ocean waters, but we also pour our sewage into those same waters. It is, when you think about it, a veritable wonder that the coast still exists at all.

People are at work all over the South, in fact, to save this wetland resource. And in the process, several of our conceptions about Southerners are coming in for close examination.

In 1972 Congress passed the Coastal Zone Management Act, largely through the efforts of Senator Ernest F. Hollings of South Carolina, a Charlestonian who had seen the wetlands of his boyhood become polluted and ravished. The act has many facets, but essentially it promotes the effective "management" of the coast (a term dearly loved by the environmental bureaucrats) by encouraging the substitution of long-term planning at the state level for the present chaos of conflicting local, state, and federal jurisdictions that frequently results in no planning at all.

One regional value affected by the act is the Southerner's presumed love for the environment. Southern people, the reasoning goes, will accept what amounts to the zoning of the coastal area because they love the coast and want, more than most other Americans, to preserve it. Another, and somewhat conflicting, proposition is the feeling that Southerners *talk* about their love for their land, but that they abuse that land terribly. Thomas M. Massengale, the North Carolina representative for the Nature Conservancy, an organization which has done a great deal (more than most elected officials) to save the seacoast and other parts of the environment, told me: "According to my own reading and experience, the South probably has less respect for the environment than any other part of the country. The South has never been concerned with the land. The early farmers mined the soil, ruined it, and moved west. The impression has always been that the land was limitless. You could always move on."

And, to get back specifically to the seacoast, there is the well-known disinclination of the coastal Southerner to enjoy being told by the government—any government—what to do with his or her land, property, or life. And then there's the profit motive: coastal landowners sometimes lose sight of their love for the environment when a land speculator comes around with an open checkbook; coastal politicians are usually eager to attract industry, even if it's not of the cleanest sort. It will be interesting to see which characteristics win out, or whether it is possible for all of them to be merged into one value that saves the coast.

Florida, which has lost twenty-five percent of its wet-lands to development in the last two decades, serves as everybody else's bad example. But the pressures of indus-try and development are strong all over the region. South Carolina not long ago established a Coastal Council, which essentially is a zoning and planning agency for the shore. "For us just to pass the bill," said an official, "is probably the most revolutionary thing since they fired on Fort Sumter."

The official made the standard comment that he hoped South Carolina wouldn't turn out like Florida. "Florida has had a hard time," he said, "because of all its develop-ment. And that means money, and money means pressure on the people who make the decisions. South Carolina hasn't had those pressures—yet, at least. Why? Consider who owns the government in South Carolina. The good old Southern boys still own it here. They aren't immune to pressures from developers, but they *do* like to fish and hunt."

While South Carolina decided to pass its legislation first and then work on its coastal plan, Georgia did the reverse.

Governor George Busbee appointed, in spring, 1976 an Advisory Council on Coastal Zone Management, and its recommendations are on their way back to him and then to the legislature. In North Carolina, one emphasis has been on public education. The state built three Marine Resources Centers along the coast. They are laboratory centers, where biologists, botanists, and others spend the summer on research projects and where high school teachers go for brush-up courses. But these labs are also educational centers for the general public. The center at Bogue Banks, for example, in the summer of 1977, organized dozens of activities, including field trips into salt marshes, photo exhibits, night snorkeling, nature walks, films, and an excellent series of lectures, and also operated a delightful public aquarium.

"People really come to see us," said Ned A. Smith, a biologist who is the resident director of the Bogue center. People—who might otherwise have come to the coast on vacations and done the traditional things like "relaxing" and "sunbathing"—were coming by at the rate of a thousand a day and discovering things they never knew about the seacoast.

"The hope," said Smith, "is that these people will go away with a new appreciation of the coastal zone, and that they'll understand how delicate it is and how badly we need to save it."

Morehead City is a year-round city, but it badly needs the dollars of the summer beach people who stop for a devilish traffic light before they turn onto the bridge across Bogue Sound. Nobody thinks of the place on the other side of the bridge as "Bogue Banks" now, although that is its name, because it doesn't look anymore like the classical North Carolina barrier islands that are named "Banks." Except for a few stretches of beach where bathers and walkers are rare, it is a highly developed sample of the Southern seacoast, full of second homes, ocean-front cottages, condominiums, high-rise motels, and a miniature golf course overrun with cement elephants and ostriches.

But avoid the bridge and stay on U.S. 70 a few minutes longer, and you'll come to Beaufort. The population thins out even more if you keep going, but Beaufort is as far away from the industry and crowdedness of the mainland as many people want to go. It was settled in 1709 and once was named Fishtown, and it hasn't changed all that much. If you went into the drugstore on the waterfront during this summer and asked for a lemonade, they'd squeeze it for you on the spot, using real lemons. The houses, many of them handsome, go down almost to the waterline, and then there's a narrow channel, Taylor Creek, that is used mostly by small craft bound for the more deserted banks.

Across Taylor Creek from Beaufort, almost literally a stone's throw away from the street that runs along the waterfront, is Carrot Island. There are no second homes, condos, or miniature golf courses on Carrot Island. There are, however, semi-wild horses there. They wander the mile-or-so length of the island grazing on its grasses. If you stand on the Beaufort waterfront long enough, you're likely to see them, in silhouette, across the channel. The horses sort of complete the transition from populated mainland to primitive coastline. And the sight of them clearly demonstrates that this is the way much of the Southern seacoast should be preserved.

The fate of Carrot Island has not always been secure, though. Several years ago a man from the mainland, Robert Clodfelter, bought the island from a British conglomerate for a relatively low price—$68,000. Clodfelter then announced that he wanted to auction the land off in five-acre parcels. The announcement struck Beaufort like an

October hurricane, for most people hadn't even known about the British conglomerate. Iva Holland, who lives in a house along the waterfront, was particularly upset.

Iva Holland was the daughter of the first physician to practice on the Outer Banks. In 1910, when she was a child, her family had moved to Beaufort. She remembers going swimming over on Bogue Banks. The bridge hadn't been built, and you had to go over by boat. When she grew up she left the quiet life of the seacoast and went to Washington, where she worked for forty years for the columnist David Lawrence. She lived in Fairfax, Virginia, which in recent years has turned from a pleasant, pastoral environment into wall-to-wall suburbia. When Iva Holland retired three years ago, she moved back to Beaufort. From her breezy house she can see across to Carrot Island and its feral horses.

"We used to call it Bird Shoals," she said. (Nautical charts still call it that.) "Fishermen dried their nets on it. Over time, the engineers dredged Taylor Creek, and they threw the spoils onto the island, building it up. Then nature brought along the grass and the scrubby trees, and a few dunes developed. Somehow the horses got there. It never occurred to me that somebody *owned* the place. I thought—a lot of people thought—that the town or the county owned it. People treated it as if it was public property. They'd go clamming over there, or picnicking." I remembered what Bob Barbee, at one time the superintendent of Cape Hatteras National Seashore, had told me years before about the *outer* Outer Banks: "The people in this region regard these islands as a *commons.*"

He meant a place where everyone may go, without challenge, without meeting harm, and without causing harm. And certainly not a place full of second homes and condos.

"We got a court order and stopped the sale," said Iva Holland. "Some of us got pretty excited about making sure it didn't happen. But a lot of people didn't get worried at all. They'd argue that you couldn't get over there, and that you couldn't build anything over there, and so there was no reason to worry about it."

Clodfelter, whom the environmentalists praised as being honorable and sympathetic, never proposed to develop the bridgeless island; only to sell it off in parcels. It was assumed by some that the logical buyers would be the adjacent homeowners along the mainland, who would want to protect their views of the shoals and seascape. "But then there was some talk about building a gondola to get people over to the island," said Holland. "People *really* got excited about *that.*"

Iva Holland and others formed the Beaufort Land Conservancy Council, and they did all the things that people do when they're confronted with an environmental crisis. They hired a lawyer and a surveyor and held meetings. "Suddenly," said Holland, who was the trustee and treasurer of the council, "Carrot Island was becoming important. It was becoming important that it *not* be developed. A lot of rumors got started—that there would be an oil tank farm there, things like that. Nobody had ever thought about it as anything except protection for the waterfront against the elements. And its scenic value. In most people's minds, it was something that was always there and that would always *be* there. But now it was being threatened."

The council asked for help from Tom Massengale at the Nature Conservancy, a non-profit national agency that solicits financial gifts and uses them to purchase "ecologically and environmentally significant land" and manage it until governmental agencies are able to do the job. Clodfelter, meantime, offered to sell the land to the Beaufort group for $400,000; later he lowered the price to $250,000, and then even lower.

But the island-lovers had trouble raising the money.

Two industries along Taylor Creek, a menhaden fish processing plant and a veneer mill, made substantial donations, but the response from local people was not overwhelming. "The people who were most active in all this," said Holland, "were furriners." Duke University, which is relatively "fur" from the coast, haggled with foundations in an effort to guarantee part of the payment. Other donations came from individuals who rarely, if ever, got to Beaufort to see the horses graze on Carrot Island, but who had read about the crisis in the newspapers.

Why hadn't the local people helped more?

"A lot of the people who live here," said Iva Holland, "have never been away from here. They haven't seen what can happen to places that are pretty and unspoiled. They say—and I heard a lot of them say this in connection with Carrot Island—'It's always been like this and it won't change.' We who've been away have seen with our own eyes what can happen to the environment."

And that is a lesson that must be learned by the South. For so long we have been blessed with a beautiful environment that, like the long, sensual, delicious season of Southern warmth, seemed to be unending. It was easy to allow bits and pieces, and then large chunks of it to disappear, to be turned into condominiums and papermills. There was always more of it where that came from, we thought. We have never considered many of our Carrot Islands to be valuable until it was too late; until someone else has recognized their value.

Carrot Island is now much closer to salvation. A financial bargain was struck that probably will insure that it stays the way it is. But other elements of the Southern environment, especially along the fragile coastline, are in grave danger. Their value has not yet been recognized by sufficiently large numbers of people—especially, by sufficiently large numbers of *local* people.

On the same front page of the *Carteret County News-Times,* which carried a story about Carrot Island that summer, there was an article about political leaders from Morehead City and the communities on Bogue Banks, the heavily developed island. The leaders were proclaiming that a new bridge to Bogue was "badly needed" for the economic development of the area.

There are no feral horses left on Bogue Banks. Only cement elephants and ostriches on a miniature golf course.

22

Common decency

My journey through the warmer regions ended late in the fall.

A half-dozen times I traveled from the crowded exile of New York City down through my native Southland, trying to discover what the South had become. Sometimes I was almost sure I had found it. But more often it was like trying to recall a dream that you know, upon awaking, is very important, but that remains elusive. I knew, or thought I knew, what I had been looking for, but I was not able to reach out and touch it; it drifted away from me like a cloud.

Back when I started, the Southland's lakes and ponds were just beginning to produce life again after a deep, painful winter. I felt the late frosts in the mountains and watched the leaves come out and turn to a fresh, clear green, and then, as the summer progressed, I watched them become darker as their youth, like ours, slowly changed to old age. Now they lay as so much mulch on the Southern ground, waiting for winter.

I witnessed some of the disastrous floods, more violent that year than most. And along with many others, I waited for the destructive hurricane of '77 that never materialized. I smelled the honeysuckle and the salt air as it warmed, and now I smelled the hardwood smoke of autumn that hung in the lowlands and mountain valleys.

The journey was almost totally serendipitous. I had no idea what I would find, and only a few vague ideas of what I was looking for. I wanted to see what had happened with race relations, of course, the preoccupation of my and earlier generations. And to examine the theory that some have advanced that the South had abandoned its culture and become absorbed into the American mainstream. And I wanted to explore the old question about whether there actually is a New South, and to see the impact of a Southerner's election as President.

I promised myself that I would ask all with whom I talked for their definition of the South, and for their lists of the qualities that were particularly Southern and that should be preserved. After a while I stopped asking because I found the people were volunteering the information. They *wanted* to talk about the South. It was as if they had kept the secret long enough, and now they needed to share it.

I found that a lot of my own biases showed through. I spent an inordinate amount of time close to the ocean and the Gulf, and I spent a lot of it in North Carolina, my home state, and I probably didn't spend enough time in the larger cities. I also found that I suffered an amazing lack of guilt over those transgressions. Some of what I heard and saw was surprising to me, and that was good, because a reporter likes to have his preconceived notions knocked to pieces every once in a while. I found that I was accumulating a certain body of fairly *positive* material.

I didn't particularly mean for that to happen. It just turned out that way. The South is quite a positive place these days. I found myself wishing that the rest of the nation could be absorbed into the Southern mainstream so we could inject a little more quality into American life. And I found myself wishing that the journey through the warmer regions didn't have to end.

The South *is* becoming more like the North, to be sure. The nationwide sameness of television, interstate highways, shopping centers, and the other roadside apparitions have seen to that. The 800-number-ization of America. And I was alarmed to see that mindless bureaucracy in the South can be just as mindless as it is in the North.

One of my trips was entirely by surface public transportation, and I found myself one midnight at the Amtrak station in Charleston, South Carolina, which is really in North Charleston, waiting for a train to take me back to New York. After a while I asked the young man behind the bulletproof window, whose name was Mike, if the train would be on time. No, he said through the defective intercom, it would be thirty minutes late.

"Were you going to announce that to us?" I asked, somewhat testily.

"Why, do you want me to?" he replied, somewhat testily.

"Well," I said, "the train's going to be late. Presumably the people here would like to know that. I know *I* sure would."

"It's *not* late," said Mike. "According to the Interstate Commerce Commission, thirty minutes isn't late."

"What about according to your brain?" I asked.

"That doesn't count," he said.

There were other disturbing scenes: the gasoline stations that refuse to accept anything but exact change or credit cards after eight P.M. because Southerners, like other Americans, perceive crime as being omnipresent; the rental-cops at the gatehouses on the coastal second-home communities, ever watchful for a visitor who doesn't "look right"; the depressing sight of able-bodied, mentally-alert young men walking around downtown Atlanta at nine in the morning drinking beer out of cans hidden in paper bags, just as they do in New York.

But the South has not lost itself yet by any means. Its most precious human asset, individualism, is still there, hiding behind, and sometimes in open combat with, the forces that would reduce us all to androids. Sometimes it comes out in language. In a restaurant washroom, there is the standard sign warning employees that they must wash their hands before returning to the kitchen. Yet here it cites not only the pertinent state law, but also "common decency." Maybe that's a characteristic that is peculiar to the South.

In Florida they were tearing down a motel. A hand-lettered sign warned passersby: "Do not block drive. Nails in area. Stupid if you do."

Andrew Lozica started working on his shrimp boat more than four years before. The logical place to build a fifty-four-foot boat was in the front yard of his house in Hobucken, North Carolina. Now the boat was almost finished, and it was bigger than the house.

"I started with two hundred pounds of stainless steel nails and eighteen hundred dollars worth of lumber," he said. Then the market went wild and everything started costing more, but he kept on going, since there really aren't too many alternatives when you've got a partially-built shrimp boat in your front yard. "I kind of hope to put it overboard by the end of the year," he said, "but even then there'll be a lot of work to do."

Andrew Lozica, who was thirty-one at that time, works in a phosphate mine from four P.M. until midnight. He started building the Shaleen, named after his daughter, because he didn't have much else to do during the mornings. "I guess you might say I got to do things different than anybody else," he said, and he went back to work on the trawler.

"The trouble with New York is that it's worn out," said Eugene Odum. He holds professorships in ecology and zoology at the University of Georgia and he is the South's, and probably the nation's, most distinguished ecologist. "It may be so rotten that the city will have to be abandoned."

He watched for my reaction, since I live and have a mortgage there. "That's not necessarily bad," he continued with sort of a scientist's detachment. "It's just age. Things get old. We can build another one on top of it, just as people have been doing for centuries."

There's another kind of rottenness in New York and in much of the non-South. It is a rottenness that comes from having done things greedily for so long, for taking and taking and taking and never putting anything back. One of the most exciting ideas I got from this journey was the notion that the South was in a position for avoiding this corruption of its body and soul.

Practically nobody talked about Jimmy Carter unless I

asked about him. It was as if he had stopped being a Southerner on the day he went into office. Or, as some suspected, as if he had never been a real Southerner to start with. Just a politician, interchangeable with all other politicians, maybe a little better than most.

An office worker answered the telephone in New York and I could tell immediately she was a Southerner. I asked her where she came from.

"Americus, Georgia," she replied. We talked a moment about the facility of the Southerner in the North to turn the accent on or off at will, depending on who was listening.

"I started letting mine show *before* Mr. Carter became president," she said. "It was about the time Boston started having trouble with its schools. Ours were integrating without any problems and theirs weren't. That's about the time I started not being ashamed of my accent."

The most satisfying discovery was that the South had lost its terrible preoccupation with race. Racism, hatred, prejudice, discrimination both blatant and subtle—they all exist in the South, and in some places where they existed in minute quantities before, they seem now to be recurring. But throughout most of the South that I saw, they prevail to a far lesser degree than ever before, and they no longer have official sanction, and these evils are now much more advanced in the rest of the nation. The South, both black and white, has entered a terribly long and dark and awful tunnel, and now it has emerged from the other side, and things will never be the same again.

A white man from rural Mississippi was active in the

movement for racial peace in the sixties. Because of his work he had to leave his home state and move to Tennessee. Each summer he would receive word—painfully delivered, for his family loved and missed him—that it would be better for his own safety if he didn't come home for the annual family reunion. His work in the Movement was well known back home. One year the word was that some of his family's neighbors had threatened to kill him if he showed up.

In the summer of 1977 the message was that it sure would be nice if he came for the reunion; that things had changed.

Along about the middle of the summer I realized that I was in the process of becoming a born-again Southerner.

The dinner at a friend's house was delicious, and the accents mellow and the humor excellent. Because I am a reporter and am allowed to pose such questions, I asked about the status of women's liberation in the Southern city, which is nameless here but which is very much like a dozen other medium-sized Southern cities.

The three women replied cautiously. One said she didn't like it "if we're talking about the thing that calls itself women's lib now." Another said she felt that *in some cases* women doing the same work as men should get the same pay.

Two of the men came on as classical chauvinist pigs and the other kept quiet. Later in the conversation it developed that all three of the women worked in meaningful jobs and contributed greatly to their family incomes. One was a supervisor in a business, one worked in a federal agency, and the third was a freelance systems analyst and computer programmer.

The sign outside Hall's Nursery and Greenhouses in Mary Esther, Florida, advertised caladiums at an unheard-of low price, and since I am a sucker for caladiums I pulled in. John Hall met me.

"I can tell you're interested in this kind of thing," he said after a few minutes. "Come on, I'll show you the place."

For an hour we walked through his greenhouses and alongside his flower beds, and Hall described the plants, many of them tropical. Occasionally he'd break off a leaf or a twig and hand it to me to smell or eat. "This is sassafras," he said. "Good for tea, and the leaves give you filé for your Creole dishes." He also had peppermint and anise and a dozen others.

As we walked, he collected shoots and sprouts in a bag. Some of them, he said, were quite rare in this country. A friend had brought many of them back from South America and propagated them in his nursery in Miami. When the unprecedented cold weather came in the winter of 1976–77, they died, because nobody in Miami had thought they'd ever need to heat their greenhouses.

At the end of our stroll I bought two caladiums and a fern. Not a spectacular purchase. John Hall handed me the plants he'd been collecting. "I can tell you like these things," he said. "It isn't right to charge money for things that grow free, especially when they're going to people who love them."

He started to say something else, hesitated, and lost his concentration. "I apologize," he said. "I was poisoned by pesticides. It makes me lose my memory sometimes." He was a very gentle man. Because I am a knee-jerk liberal, I have always reacted with as much horror as the next person to the word "pesticide." From that moment on it meant something even worse to me.

"There are some aspects of Southerners," said Eugene Odum, "that help give me optimism about the job we have to do on the environment. There's the Southerner's love for the outdoors and nature. There is, I think, a little less materialism in the Southerner—but this seems to be changing, and I'm afraid the Southerner's materialism is growing.

". . . The Southerner is becoming more like the American in general. But at the moment the good qualities exist in sufficient quantity. We've seen how the Southerner reacts. A few years ago we had a big controversy in Georgia over a plan to disturb the salt marshes for phosphate mining. Those of us who thought the marshes shouldn't be disturbed figured at first that we'd have a pretty tough time convincing the governor and the legislature. But it turned out that everybody wanted to protect the marshes—poor people, rich people, everybody. The legislators told me they were surprised at the number of letters they got.

"I think the biggest job we need to do now is the sort of job we did on race. Only this time we must do it on the environment. In a way, doing this on the environment is more important than doing it on race. You can have failures from time to time in human relations and recover from them, but you can't have any failures in the environment. There's just no second chance."

I thought about Odum's comments for a long time. The South's future is its environment. Take away the other qualities that people usually list when they try to define the South—its food, its way of talking, its slower pace, even its manners—and you'd still have something that you can pretty much call *the South*. We have already taken away what we once considered the region's most important identifying characteristic, its institutionalized racism, and it remains the South.

But take away the environment of the South and you might as well have New Jersey.

A quotation from Joel Fleishman, a former classmate of mine, who, as we have seen before, has lived in the North and now is at Duke University: "There is a devotion to *place* in the South—you see it a lot in the literature—that I don't think has diminished. And a kind of informality. And an openness and warmth about relationships. And that's why, I think, most of the people I know here are fairly happy people, and most of the people I know in New York are *not* particularly happy people."

Quotation from Dirk Frankenberg, a professor of marine science at Chapel Hill, who was brought up in Massachusetts but who considers himself now a Southerner: "Much of the South is just waiting for things to happen. You can almost feel the anticipation. It's a feeling that *we're about to get ours.*"

Quotation from a man who pulled in next to me at a rest stop on Interstate 85 late one January night, when it was very cold: "I'm headed for Louisiana. From Philadelphia. Ain't going to stop until I get warm again. I'm going *home.*"

Quotation from Ned Smith, who runs the coastal laboratory on Bogue Banks: "Slowly the South is being discovered. People are moving here from places that have made mistakes, and those people don't want to make those mistakes again."

Quotation from a middle-aged black woman, a para-professional at a Veterans' Administration hospital in the South, who was riding the Southern Crescent from New York down toward Atlanta during a long, sleepless night: "My son's in the theater in New York City. After he'd been there a while he told me, 'Momma, don't let anybody talk bad about the South. Don't let them say the South's worse than the North, 'cause it isn't.' "

Quotation from Terry Moore, a young black man from Conway, South Carolina, who works as a doffer in a yarn mill. (He flips empty spindles off the machine and puts full ones on. The machine holds two hundred sixty spindles. "I love my work, man," he said.) "This is nice, man. The races are getting together, man. It's a whole lot different. The way things are right now, we are considered as one. The whites are a part of me. And I am a part of them. We know each other better here than we would in the North. People getting together, people being together. It's beautiful."

Exchange with a woman whose badge said "Head Cashier" in a Winn-Dixie supermarket in Washington, North Carolina:

"I've got some deposit bottles here. Where do I put them?"

"Just put them there with the others and tell me or the other cashier when you go through the checkout how many you brought in."

"You mean you'll take my word on how many?"

"Sure. You're in the South now."